7 Secrets to Achieving Rapid Growth in Your Remodeling Business...

And How You Can Crush it Online

Ryan Paul Adams

© 2013, 2015 Ryan Paul Adams
Published by PME 360
info@pme360.com

www.PME360.com

What People Have to Say About Ryan Paul Adams and PME 360

"PME 360 is a marketing company unlike any other PPC, SEO, or online marketing agency I have met thus far. What they are doing with my website is literally taking my breath away.

They have developed several resources for me including a new guide, landing pages, and full email nurturing sequence that explains my business and services better than anything I have attempted before. This is going to be HUGE!!

You should not make a final decision on hiring anyone to help with your marketing until you check these guys out. Hands down, they are the most professional and comprehensive company I have dealt with for my website needs and for online lead management. Absolutely awesome. That is all I can say!"

Jennifer Bylo
President
Bay State Re-Bath

"I take our marketing very seriously because it defines the image that people have of you and your company. It is very difficult to find someone that cares as much as you do when it comes to marketing your company, but I feel like I've found my guy.

Ryan Paul Adams has done a wonderful job with our online marketing and the number of leads we've gotten from the internet has increased 67% over last year.

We have used 4 or 5 different SEO/SEM website companies in the past and some did more harm than good. Ryan is an ethical guy that wants to do things the right way, hiring Ryan and his team at PME 360 has been a great decision."

TJ Elbert
General Manager
Elbert Construction

"At the Builders Show in Las Vegas this past year, I picked up a book titled "7 Secrets To Achieving Rapid Growth in Your Remodeling Business: And How You Can Crush It Online" by Ryan Paul Adams. The book opened my eyes to a whole new world of marketing I have not seen before in my industry. It also introduced me to a company that could handle this new world for me. I've always

struggled with the online/marketing needs of my company. My time is limited as I take care of the day to day needs of my company. In regards to marketing, I would do a little here and a little there but only when I had time and work was slow.

After interviewing and researching PME360 thoroughly, I decided to partner with them. And I don't use the term "partner" loosely. I do feel like they are partners in my business and are truly concerned with the lead generation process and in other aspects of my company's marketing and branding campaigns.

One thing I should make you aware of is that if you aren't in a position to grow and grow fast, you need to think twice about hiring them. Over the past 4 months, we have had to bring on 5 new administrative staff members to accommodate our increasing market share. My phone rings several times a day and I usually get several internet leads a day. It has gotten so busy that I have begun selling the leads that I can't handle to smaller outfits in my area.

My experience has been a profitable one and I would recommend them to any other remodeling company (as long as you aren't in the Salt Lake Valley)."

Todd Cella
Sales Manager/CEO
Utah Basement Kitchen and Bath

"As many of us in the industry can relate, we find ourselves wearing too many hats and spreading our time too thin. There are only so many hours in the day and I found myself working too much to keep up with everything that is involved in helping to run a business, including marketing.

Obviously, marketing is one important aspect in the success of any business. It lays a firm foundation by spreading the message of who you are and what you do and how you go about doing it. I learned long ago that it is equally, if not more important to market your business during the busy times versus waiting until things slow down.

Thankfully we were approached by Ryan and his team to see if we would be a good fit for each other. Initially, my only worry was "losing control" of our marketing efforts as I truly believed that only I, or we know our business well enough to market it. However, what I have found is we always have input on areas to focus on and I have regular contact with the PME 360 team to see if everyone is on the same page.

I believe we are now promoting a more consistent, more professional image of our company and our services using the experience of PME 360. And, as a result, I am more focused on helping to run and grow our business without the weight of also marketing it. I am now working less hours and *the results have been fantastic.*

Jason M Gettum, CGR
Vice President
Gettum Associates

"We started using PME 360 about two years ago, with a website re-design and SEO package. Our business doubled from the previous year. This past spring we did a SEO, website tune-up and went with their Power Local Pro product. And within two weeks of launching, besides increasing our customer call-ins, we received several calls from dealers, manufactures and even our competition asking us "what are you doing differently with your web marketing".

PME360 has greatly increased our web presence, boosted our ratings, and the phone and e-mails are coming in. We are extremely happy with the level of service, their knowledge of their industry, and performance of their products. We are excited about what they done for us, and what they currently do for us. You can bet that they are crucial piece of our marketing as we plan to take our business to the next level!!!"

Jim Gehm
VP of sales and marketing
Holmes Custom Renovations LLC

"For Home Remodeling companies looking to cut through the clutter of online marketing, SEO, local search, etc. – this quick read is perfect for you. Ryan knows his stuff and you'll find his very specific, clear, and actionable advice extremely valuable. Remodeling companies need to take improving their web presence seriously and this book is a perfect place to start."

Kyle Hunt
CEO/Consultant
Remodel Your Marketing

To my wife for supporting me through this entire process and talking me off the ledge when I needed it.

And to my parents for showing me the way.

I wouldn't be where I am without all of you.

And finally to my 3 kids for reminding me that there is more to life than working. They teach me to stop and appreciate the little things everyday.

Contents

Introduction

This book has been building in my mind for years. It stemmed from my 15-plus years in the remodeling business facing all the ups and downs of that world. During a substantial part of that time, I became immersed in marketing for my business simply because I felt it would be the best way to get and retain clients.

I also created a marketing agency dedicated to helping SMB (small to medium sized businesses) remodelers like you discover the incredibly effective marketing systems and techniques that I have learned. Techniques and strategies that, if executed properly, will lead you into a world of a growing clientele and substantially increased revenues, which in turn, will take you to the land of dreams fulfilled.

While an easy read this book does not do fluff. I wrote it so you could take away concrete actions and time tested business and marketing strategies that work. And most importantly, develop a mindset that prepares you for success. You will get there if you use these seven strategies that are geared to the rapid growth of your business.

Be ready to achieve!

Ryan Paul Adams

"Not all of them were successful ventures, but I have remained an entrepreneur for most of my life. I have taken all kinds of my ideas and tested them in the real world. Some didn't work, but the ones that did, well..."
- Ryan Paul Adams

Before You Read This Book -
An Offer for You and Why Most Remodeling Businesses Fail

The last thing I want you to do is to get overwhelmed with the information in this book and become paralyzed and do nothing. I am giving you a ton of information in this book and holding nothing back. But before you begin reading this book, you need to understand something very important about why most remodeling businesses FAIL.

They FAIL because they have **NO MARKETING STRATEGY**. They have taken all of this time and effort setting up the service(s) and how to deliver those services and how to get paid for those services, but they have spent little time figuring out a marketing strategy with the express goal of attracting IDEAL new clients. The key here being "IDEAL"client, and not just any client.

Can you answer the following about your business?

- Who is your ideal prospect? (Hint: It's not everyone.)

- What is the best way to ATTRACT your ideal prospect to you?

- How is your business different from your top competitors?

- What can you guarantee that is unlike any other competitor?

- Why are you in business, and what is the long term vision for your business?

If you cannot answer the previous questions easily, this book can definitely help you.

And once you are done reading this book, you have 2 options:

1) You Implement the Information Immediately and Need No Further Help.

2) You Need More Help Putting Together a Strategy and Understanding the Concepts.

Would You Like ME to Help You ATTRACT Your Ideal Client, Elminate Bad Prospects, and INCREASE Profits Instantly….for FREE?

Get a Free 30-Minute Marketing Strategy Session and Marketing Blueprint Template ….For a Limited Time!

Most business owners need at least a little bit of help understanding the concepts in this book and that's why for a *Limited Time*, my team and I are offering a **Free 30-Minute Strategy Session** to help you build an initial marketing system that is proven to get dramatic results.

There is no charge and no catch to do this but you must qualify for the session. Please visit www.PME360.com/invitation today to learn more and schedule your complimentary marketing blueprint strategy call with me.

CHAPTER ZERO:
Preparing for Quantam Growth and Adopting the Entrepreneurial Mindset

Why do I have a Chapter ZERO? Chapter ZERO was added because before we can add on any strategies or tactics, we need to start at ground zero. And ground zero in this scenario is all about improving your mindset. Without the proper mindset you cannot add the other 7 Secrets on top of it. The old ways of doing business are DEAD and I need you to want to change for the rest of this to have any chance of working.

The opportunity to absolutely dominate your local remodeling market is still wide open in every major geographic area across the US and Canada, yet so many remodeling businesses struggle immensely each and every year. This is largely due to the fact that most remodeling businesses focus (or get lost in) on production and largely ignore marketing.

After spending over 15 years in this industry as a contractor, and meeting countless remodelers, home builders, and contractors, I think I have discovered why so many remodeling businesses struggle.

Approximately 95% (my estimate) of remodeling and home improvement oriented businesses spend 80% of their time on the "inside" of their business when 80% should be spent on marketing and sales. The remaining 20% is spent on estimates and trying to land the next project when you need it. Very little effort or attention is invested in making sure you services are finding people who want them.

I call this being "bottom heavy" – where you are so overwhelmed with day-to-day production issues (getting work done) and primarily an inside focused business that you completely ignore the top (lead generation/marketing). Let's face it, most remodeling business owners didn't get into this business because they wanted to run a successful business.

They started their business because they loved their craft and then they wonder why 15 years later they are still stuck in the same place they were when they started - frustrated, stressed out, and not making the kind of money they set out to make.

To get un-stuck you need to start running your business as if you were preparing to sell it. Even if you have no plans on selling it, having the mindset that you are running a business that will be sold someday will start to change how you behave within your business almost immediately.

Adopting an entrepreneurial mindset will allow you to start thinking like an entrepreneur and stop acting like a tradesman or woman. If you are going to sell your business you need to start with marketing and your actual services (getting the jobs done) need to take a back seat. And before you throw this book in the trash because of what I just said, let me explain...

Business Success is NOT About Having the Best Service, It's About Finding Enough of The Right People Who Want What You Have to Offer

Most contractors start their business and become obsessed with making sure they have the best service on the planet. I am guilty of this to some extent but one of the reasons I had success early on in the remodeling and home building industry was the fact that I wasn't a craftsman.

I had no interest in being a carpenter or a contractor who worked on the job. My mind didn't work like that, and I purposely avoiding learning too much about physically doing the work so I wouldn't end up stuck.

I wanted to run a business and advice I received early on from my grandfather confirmed for me that I was on the right path. I will never forget what he said - *"You do not want to be the guy 'doing the work,' you want to be the guy telling others to do the work, and eventually you want to hire someone that you can tell to tell them to do the work. That is the only way you can build something great."* That "something great" he referred to was the business – not the projects we were building.

Most contractors spend an incredible amount of time focusing on the wrong things, hoping and praying that enough people hire them when they open their doors. *"If I do great work, people will notice and I will be so busy I cannot keep* up. *The money will really start to come in. I just need to make sure I perfect my services."*

The type of business owner I described above will waste years of their life and the majority of their effort perfecting their service but neglect to get their services out in front of enough of the right people. They will consistently delay taking any kind of action to improve their situation by continually telling themselves that they cannot possibly invest in marketing and getting new jobs because they simply cannot handle it.

Do not get me wrong, I want you to have the best service you can possibly provide, but not at the expense of getting new business.

"I cannot possibly get focus on marketing ahead of my services. Because...
"I do not have the money"
"I do not have the time"
"Advertising has never worked for me"
"I have so many issues with _____(fill in the blank)"
"My books are a mess!"
"I cannot take on any more jobs, I am already overloaded"

Sound about right? I hate to be the bearer of bad news but these excuses need to stop and a new mindset has to enter your consciousness.

It starts with every remodeling business shifting from a production related service first mindset (getting the jobs done) to an entrepreneurial mindset that starts with marketing. This has to begin with the owner of the business making a commitment today to marketing and that in turn will help you find enough of the right people who want to pay you money for the services you provide.

You cannot sell a job that you do not have a lead for, and you cannot produce the work if you do not have the job. It all leads back to getting your marketing strategy and marketing funnel (lead generation) in place first, which will lead to success faster than doing it the other way around. This does not mean you ignore your existing clients and jobs; however, you must free up some of your time, effort, and money to focus on marketing moving forward or you put your business at risk.

Every time I focused my efforts on marketing and being more entrepreneurial, I could increase sales 25%, 50%, and even more in a very short period of time. Something had to change and that change had to come from a better mindset.

You MUST shift your focus to marketing with everything else being secondary if you want to survive and grow a real business. When you have a marketing funnel and marketing system that produces real jobs over and over again, you have cash. When you have cash, you can hire good people to solve other big problems in your business.

Big Players Are Entering the Remodeling Market and Are Gobbling Up Market Share

My biggest concern for the small-medium sized remodeling and home improvement business is that there are bigger and better companies entering the remodeling space each and every year who are marketing focused and go after each market very aggressively. They are entrepreneurial and marketing focused companies that can quickly put you out of business if you do not make some changes. And you cannot sell a prospect that doesn't exist so focusing on selling ahead of marketing doesn't make any sense either.

Scott DeGarmo said it best in an issue of *Success Magazine*: *"The big money goes to those companies with superior marketing operations. Entrepreneurial companies of today must evolve from being sales oriented to being marketing oriented in order to now win the consumer."*[1]

Now, I do not want to be all doom and gloom here and this isn't meant to scare you, but you really do need to put a plan into action sooner than later and shift your focus now. The days of being the only one in town that does what you do is over.

More choices exist than ever before and with search engines making it so easy to research, qualify, and validate a business faster than ever before, you must have exceptional marketing above all else. Relying solely on architects, designers, and referrals for business is extremely dangerous for the future of your business, but this should be part of an overall marketing system.

Most remodeling businesses do not have exceptional marketing. Most remodelers do not have anything that even resembles a marketing message or a plan of attack. I get it...they are busy. Busy putting out fires every day and sixty and seventy hour work weeks are the norm. They wonder why they do what they do each and every day and pray for an easier way.

There are answers to these problems and the only viable way to get real freedom in your business and survive is to grow. Or to make the business so simple that it can run and thrive without the owner, and the service is in such high demand that people constantly seek you out every day for those services.

Billions in remodeling and home improvement services and products are sold each year and growing a very steady rate. If you honestly believe in yourself and the service you are offering, shouldn't you be looking to get as many of the "right" NEW clients as you can possibly handle? And if you cannot afford $1,000, $3,000, $5,000 or more to invest in marketing and to make people aware of your business each month to acquire new remodeling clients, isn't that a problem you need to solve sooner than later?

Getting Stuff Done vs Getting Your Message Out There

You cannot spend all of your time developing the inside of your business (production, sales, and systems) and neglect the outside (marketing). At some point the inside and outside of your business have to match up and preferably the outside (awareness of your business in your local market) will grow larger than you can handle. And when it does, watch out! But right now you are probably very lopsided and bottom heavy when you need to be top heavy. You can always work towards figuring out how you are going to get the services done as you go.

A new contract and a deposit from a client is a great motivator and will help you figure out how to get the work done. You can have the greatest service in the world but if few people know about it, you are in BIG TROUBLE. Most remodeling businesses deliver a great service but struggle to delegate to others on the production end.

You cannot do everything yourself and there are plenty of smart, skilled people out there that can help you get projects done. If you are making lots of mistakes and finding it difficult to hire, simplify your services so that you can succeed now. If you are struggling on the production end, your services are too complicated and you will continue to struggle. That will not change overnight. Stop doing what you are doing and start making some changes.

In the meantime, get a marketing system in place that can start moving you towards steady growth and profits so that you can hire better people to help you through your problems. You cannot grow if you do not have new projects and you cannot hire the next project manager or "internal" staff unless you have steady revenue flowing in all the time.

The answer is Marketing!

Before we dive into the *7 Secrets to Achieving Rapid Growth in Your Remodeling Business*, I want to share with you a letter I wrote recently to a potential client of mine who has struggled in the remodeling industry for over 15+ years.

He was frustrated, stressed out, working over 70 hours a week, and making less than $15/hour for his efforts. After spending about an hour with him in a strategy session, we uncovered some key things that would help him grow and get out of the chaos that he was creating.

He desperately needed more business and new revenue which in turn would help him figure out his other issues in his business. But he hesitated and wanted to find every excuse he could come up with to not take action and get his business out there in front of the right people. He was stuck. He could not fathom how he was supposed to take on new business when he was already working as much as he was. This made him very uncomfortable and he did not become a client of mine.

I left him with this letter and I hoped it would at least ignite something inside of him to where he could take action even if it was not with me.

"Hi Fred,

I can see that in your mind the "timing just isn't right." But after 15-years in your business can you honestly say that timing is ever good to do anything important? Important decisions are always difficult and uncomfortable and it is very easy to find countless reasons (excuses?) to NOT take action. You mentioned that in "3-4 months" you might be in a better place to start marketing your business, but I challenge you to really look deep down inside yourself and find if that is fact or fiction.

We become paralyzed when having to make important decisions. When people have the mindset of waiting for someday or some future point in life to make important decisions, they paralyze and stunt their potential growth. As you know, I am all about helping people grow their business which goes hand in hand with improving their quality of life. No perfect situation or scenario exists to take action. We must take action when we are faced with big decisions and find ways to solve our problems when they arise. Nothing will change unless we do something to force that change.

I understand you are struggling on the production end of things and I can certainly help you figure some of this out. While I cannot solve all of your problems on the production end, having us involved solving your biggest problem, getting new clients, I can definitely help you solve that now.

This is priority #1 and I know it feels like putting out the other fires in your business should be your top priority, but it isn't. The sooner you get complete control over your marketing and generate a steady influx of new revenue from new projects, you can then solve your other problems. I see this as the only way you can really be in a different place in 3-4 months.

Why? Because if you are not marketing and driving new business, and focused on new client generation, you are not using your entrepreneurial mind. You are still operating as a technician. When you get control over your marketing and make this a priority your business will change and so will your life. But without this focus and a good team behind you that can hold you accountable, I am afraid you will be in the same position you are in 3 or 4 months from now.

It sounds backward, but you **NEED** to focus on your marketing and make this a priority whether you do this yourself, hire someone in-house, or hire someone like myself and my team. Production is really secondary...or at least the effort spent on both need to match up somewhat. Production is important but it is not the most important thing (believe me I know what you are going through as I have struggled with this for years!). You will figure out the production end as you continue to work through the jobs and we can help you build some systems that will make things easier in the short term and the long term.

Right now you are so bottom heavy with production issues and lack the lead flow and cash flow to hire the right people to help you solve other problems. If you do not get more jobs and more revenue, how are you going to solve your production issues? Working more hours is not an option as I can tell you are nearing burn out as it is. Typically you need cash to solve this problem and I do not typically recommend that you go out and borrow a lot of money to do this unless you have a great plan in place. Your cash increase from marketing is what is going to solve your production issues, not the other way around.

If you can simplify your service, I know you can find good people who can follow instructions to get the production end of things done. And with a couple more $50k, $100k, and $200k jobs, you would be able to hire some additional high quality A and B Players and develop better systems.

You need to do what you feel is best and that is part of being the boss. Making tough decisions isn't easy but it is part of our job as leaders to do this. You have some options here, but whatever you do, please do not ignore your marketing any longer. Do something today to make it better and sooner than later your business will change for the better.

I am here if you need some help and I see a lot of potential for you and your business. You have a great reputation and solid foundation on the production end. If you want my help, I know I can get you to where you want to go if you are willing to put in some effort and stay in the fight."

Sincerely,
Ryan

More often than not, most marketing and advertising doesn't work for small to medium sized businesses, and this fact might create some hesitation in people to take action. We have all been burned. If you take a look at all the money being spent on advertising most of it delivers very little if anything at all for the small business. Mostly this is due to the fact that most SMB's have no clue how to market and who to trust.

This book is going to dive into the most important marketing you can do in today's new economy, and that is online marketing. Having a great online marketing system will lay the proper foundation for any other marketing you do.

Ten Success Tips from Remodelers Who Get it (The Success Mindset)

As some of you may know, I have been entrenched in the contracting industry my entire life. It's in my blood and my family's blood. I have always felt that I bring a very unique perspective that very few marketing and business consultants can offer this industry. But this isn't a hobby for me and that is not the sole reason why I love home remodeling.

I have felt for a while now that the home remodeling business was on the verge of exploding. You wouldn't know that from 95% of the remodeling contractors out there, but the minority, the 5% of business owners who "get it", paint a very different picture.

They have been telling me for some time now that their businesses are booming...record growth, more leads then they can handle, better quality deals, they're hiring more people, etc.

These remodeling businesses, the ones in the minority, have ten things in common:

1. They have good quality services and good reputations – off and online.
2. They want to grow (This is really important!) and possess a growth mentality.
3. They are fairly well focused and not trying to do too much.

4. They are open to listening to outside consultants and experts in areas where they are weakest.
5. They implement and execute a local internet marketing strategy including reputation marketing (by outsourcing it or doing it themselves).
6. They tapped into a marketing system that allowed them to consistently generate leads and new projects year round.
7. They are really good at getting back to people quickly.
8. They are NOT the ones doing the work.
9. They are really good at delegating and building systems.
10. They believe they are the best in the world at what they do.

What I am hearing from them is all positive. They aren't complaining about the economy and their businesses are thriving. They claim this is in large part because of strong online and offline marketing and applying many of the strategies discussed in this book.

Sounds simple enough, right? Maybe it is, maybe it isn't. That ultimately depends on what type of person you are and your ability to execute the strategies listed. But those are some of the common denominators that I am seeing that could be directly attributed to their growth...and in an economy that most people considered one of the worst ever.

Remodeling Markets are Ramping Up

People are settling into their homes for the long haul versus building or buying a new home. Baby boomers are inheriting billions and reinvesting in their homes. The lending environment is improving, and confidence is increasing while home owners are adding value back into their homes.

The combination of events is a recipe for explosive growth!

For example, baby boomers are poised to infuse about $13 trillion in new money back into the market. Guess where they are going to spend a large portion of this? You got it, back in their homes modifying them for comfort and aging-in-place living.

Consider this encouraging data about the remodeling industry (following page):

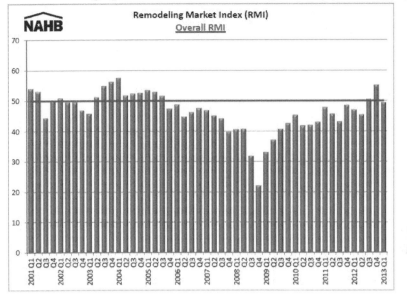

- *The graph is trending upward. From the National Association of Home Builders.[2]*
- *For the first time since housing's bubble burst, we're going into a building season in which close to a third of the U.S. metro areas are showing the most favorable economic fundamentals in nearly a decade. From MetroStudy for Remodeling Magazine.[3]*
- *The Remodeling Market Index hit 50, meaning that more contractors are reporting higher activity than lower, compared with three months ago. From Consumer Reports.[4]*

Traditionally, remodeling companies are not great marketers, In fact, most lack even basic business systems. But those remodeling companies who put in the work and focus, become great at selling what they are best at, and re-invest in their businesses (great marketing, reputation management, improve business systems, automate processes, etc.) are poised to be sitting on top of lucrative enterprises over the next few years.

Why I Love Online Marketing and Search Engines for Remodeling Businesses

Local online searches are exploding and the remodeling industry is on the verge of reaping the benefits of that explosive growth. Managed aggressively, this makes the smart local remodeling business owners very wealthy while the rest will still be complaining about the economy. And honestly, I do not even think it will be that difficult for a lot of remodeling companies to generate wealth in their businesses. Especially the ones that are one-trick ponies (window installers, roofers, siding installation, etc.) who market themselves well online and stay focused.

Search engines give your prospects full control over how they are marketed to because they put the power of choice in their hands. As consumers, we are bombarded with marketing messages and have grown accustomed to ignoring 99% of marketing. We have all learned to tune out most of them because it's just too much information for one human being to absorb.

But with search engines, it's different. We (the consumers) control what marketing information we want to receive by telling Google (or Yahoo and Bing) what we are interested in. At this stage, the prospect is in full control so you need to have a formidable web presence to get their attention and that includes:

- A Modern Website that is Mobile Responsive
- A Great Front End Offer (Ex: Guide or Catalog) to Capture Leads
- Reviews on a Variety of Review Sites (like Yelp)
- Updated Social Profiles
- Lots of Accurate Local Listings
- Content – Blog, Press Releases, Videos

The point is, you need to be everywhere your prospects are. Think about how you start your research process online to find restaurants, information, local businesses, or products you potentially want to use. If you are like most people, you start off with a general idea of what you are looking for.

How Prospects Search For You

Let's take an example of doing a search for a siding contractor: You would start with an online search at Google (80% of your market on average) with "siding contractor + area they live" or "siding installer" "siding company". These screen shots show the SERP (Search Engine Results Page) from a search for siding contractors in Chicago:

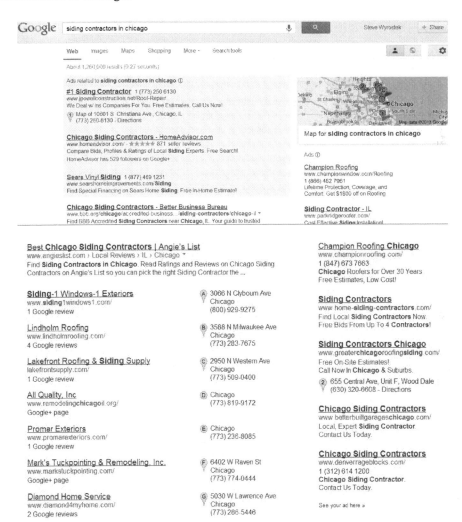

You are going to get a variety of listings in the SERP. Some searches will generate only organic search results. Others (like this one) will produce:

- Google + Map results (near the top with the map)
- Paid listings (top and sides) called PPCs (Pay Per Clicks)
- Local directory listings
- Reviews, social media results, articles, blog posts, videos
- Actual company sites that install siding

The search engines #1 goal is to provide a great and informative experience for its users. That is how Google ultimately makes money. The best way to do that is to provide relevant information related to your search with a variety of content for you to gather information from. That's why you rarely see one site dominate the entire 1st page of Google for a term like the one above, but it can happen, if you are crafty.

Your customers are everywhere online and they do not rely on one site to find a company or one source (social, directories, search engines, etc.) to make a final decision. Google is the #1 search engine on the internet. It's where 80% of your market will start their research, but not necessarily where they make the final buying decision. Pay attention to what I just told you! Once the prospect narrows down their list of potential companies to work with, they begin the process of making sure the business is reputable by reading information online about the contractor's business.

You need to have a web presence beyond just your main website.

At any stage of this research and vetting process you can lose a prospect for a multitude of reasons. Do not give them any reasons to go with your competitor! Be everywhere they are, provide great information and a variety of content. Especially, make it easy for them to say YES and take the next steps with you (Free Estimate, Consultation, Guide Book, Standards Guide, Project Review, etc.).

Consciously or not we are all disqualifying potential businesses at a speed never before seen in the history of mankind. You only get a few seconds to make a great first impression. To hold a precious potential customer after that, you better have updated content in your blog, updated information on your Facebook Fan Page, 10+ additional web properties that mention your company, and at least a couple of reviews and testimonials somewhere online. Shoot for at least 10 reviews online to start on at least 2 or 3 review sites.

If you do not, you can kiss about 80% of your interested visitors goodbye. Gone forever.

Sure, this is a lot of work, but the good news is that so few of your remodeling competitors will ever take action to put marketing systems in place that the opportunity to dominate online is wide open.

Remember, your competition is typically terrible at marketing their business. The door is wide open in every city and town across the country. Implement, focus, attack and you will succeed. My clients are proof of that!

"But My Business is 100% Based on Referrals"

Before I get into the specifics of what you exactly need to do, I want to clear something up for all the business owners reading this that say "But my business is 100% generated by referrals, I do not need this stuff!"

First of all, NO local remodeling service business should rely 100% on referrals. It is not scalable and it's a very difficult business model to predict. If you have any dreams of selling the business you created some day, you better start generating leads from sources outside of the people and clients who already know you. You need referrals but also you need to market to past clients and the people they refer to you. Do not just sit back and think that good referrals are going to happen automatically.

Second, if you are offering such a great service that word of mouth is all you have needed to survive to this point, now might be the perfect time to thrive! Or do you NOT want to make any more money? (Maybe you cannot handle growing your business but that's a totally different issue.)

Third, you are losing business because you do not exist online or your web presence is so poor. This I can 100% guarantee. Countless times, I personally have shied away from engaging with local businesses that were referred to me by people I trust because their web presence was terrible or the information I found was not giving me a warm, fuzzy feeling.

You need reviews, you need a website, and you need lots of good information online about your company to capture all your referral business. Do not assume that you are capturing all your referral business properly. You probably aren't if you are not doing any of what I am about to share.

The Growth Mentality

None of what I am about to teach you matters at all if you do not have the mentality for growth. Far too many business owners aren't comfortable with making more money and experiencing true success in their business. Growth is good. Growth is necessary. You have to want it because it will not come to you on its own.

Staying where you are right now is not good. It never is. I am not suggesting you cannot ever be happy with what you have accomplished, but if you stay put, you are putting your business at risk. You can only stay put and not grow or be innovative if you can be guaranteed by your top competitors that they will do the same. Go and ask them. Get them all in the same room or on a conference call if you can. If, at that meeting, you can all agree that you won't try and steal market share from each other, that none of you will try and improve your service, that none of you will try and improve your marketing and sales strategies or improve your systems, then do not worry about the rest of this book. You are fine to stay where you are.

Business is not static. It's dynamic. It's vibrant. It moves. Same goes for marketing. The remodeling industry changes all the time. To compete you need to be aggressive with your knowledge, hire the right people and consultants, and stay just a few steps ahead to determine where the industry is going. If you sit back, I guarantee you there are remodeling businesses that are hiring people like me, David Mihm, Perry Marshall, and Dan Kennedy to look for innovative, cutting-edge ways to market and grow their enterprises.

If you aren't someone who likes to learn and stay on top of your industry, if you aren't immersed, then you probably aren't in the right business. Surround yourself with the best possible people you can for free and those that you need to pay, pay well. The best people do not work for $15 per hour so if you aren't growing you may need to look at the team around you first. Do not hire "cheap" people it will hurt you more times than help.

You cannot get out of the craziness that is your business without growing. Growth allows you to hire more people, get stuff off your plate, re-invest in your product/service, and achieve your big dream, whatever that may be. To hire or outsource you need cash and using revenue that you produce to grow is a more comfortable way to grow your business than borrowing from any source. You may need some initial funds to get going and get marketing, but I do not advocate borrowing a lot if you can avoid it.

Plain and simple – If you do not grow, your competitors will. That will leave you and your business at risk. You have to market yourself and your business. You need to cultivate a strong online presence. You do not have a choice any longer. Barely monitoring a neglected website from five years ago and having little or no other web presence isn't going to cut it.

The time to shift from being production focused to marketing focused is **now**. Enjoy my 7 Secrets and hopefully in a few hours the secret will be out and in your brain forever and then implemented in your business.

"Delaying the Sale" Will Actually Help You Attract, Qualify, Prepare, and Close Better Clients At a Premium Price

Unless you are selling some kind of low cost, instant need, quick fix remodeling service, you need to strongly consider slowing down the sales process. In fact, delaying your sales process can help you dramatically improve your entire business.

If you need to sell something today to survive, this is NOT for you. And if this is in fact your current situation, or the kind of pressure you put on your sales people, you will not succeed for long in today's highly competitive marketplace.

Great marketing doesn't have to take a lifetime to integrate into your business, but it does take a full understanding, commitment, and investment of both time and money to get it right. And you need to start by actually taking a step back in your sales process to take 10 steps forward.

Position Yourself as the Local Remodeling "Expert"
To properly position yourself as the remodeling expert in your local market you absolutely must lead with something of value before you do any kind of consultation or estimate.

You need to delay the sale so that you can grow your remodeling business and get more out of the marketing and awareness you are creating. And the most effective way to delay the sale is to offer a lower barrier to entry for your prospects to enter into your marketing and sales funnel.

This may seem like a completely foreign concept to some but it is 100% true for just about every remodeling business on the planet that is actively trying to sell high ticket, premium remodeling services in competitive markets.

You may have heard of direct response marketing in the past and may or may not understand the significance of this type of marketing strategy, but you will after you read the rest of this. Direct response marketing is at its very core a marketing strategy built around delaying the sale with an attractive front end, low barrier to entry offer (ex: Free Info Kit, Free Design Kit, 7 Things You Should Know Guide).

You can find these kinds of direct response offers in most industries and I am confident you would see a bunch of these offers if you turn on the television tonight, but very few remodeling companies use this strategy (except for my clients I very rarely see direct response marketing in the remodeling industry).

IF you are the only game in town, by all means go straight for the sale. Go directly for the estimate each and every time and don't delay anything! But I don't know of anyone for whom this is the case.

IF you are in competition with two or more businesses on every potential sale **YOU ABSOLUTELY MUST DIFFERENTIATE** and learn how to "show up like no one else" or you risk having to compete on price….or worse, having to work with a less than ideal client just to keep your doors open.

But How You Ask Can I Differentiate and Delay the Sale?

In most cases, the power of delaying the sale will actually help you ATTRACT prospects to you that are properly qualified and fully prepared to do business with you and only you. Not always, but you stand a much better chance of crushing it in your local market with this strategy than anything else you try.

Just about anyone can create awareness for their business using marketing. There are a number of ways to drive traffic and leads and a million and one companies offer these kinds of services. You have probably tried a couple of "seo" or "ppc" companies and even dabbled with some direct mail and you have probably gotten some leads from it.

But the real magic in marketing doesn't come from driving the initial awareness. This is the mistake that 99% of business owners make is that they do not understand this concept. The REAL MAGIC happens after the initial awareness and lead is captured and how this prospect comes to know, like, and eventually (if you do this correctly) TRUST YOU.

If done correctly, this will also give you the best opportunity to charge more for the exact same services you offer today. And, most importantly, it stops your prospect from needing to "think it over" or "I am going to call 3 or 4 other remodelers to get quotes."

Slowing Down the Sales Process Allows You to Scale Quicker

Slowing down the sales process can be done by simply marketing differently. Instead of leading with a free estimate or free consultation, instead give your prospect something of value (free guide, book, cd, info kit, etc) before you do any kind of estimate or consultation. And give this to them way before they ever talk to you.

Your prospect isn't ready for you to come out to their house and sell them. You can certainly try to do it that way and you will get some sales. You have probably been doing it this way for years and have had some success. But if you stop and think about it....what do your prospects really know about you at this point IF they aren't a referral?

And even if they are a referral, how likely are they to just buy from you without doing some research first? Have you had a chance to educate them as to why you are better or different than your top 10 competitors?

With Lead Engine we solve this problem for you and highly encourage you to even take this a step further by physically mailing something to your prospects ahead of a sales conversation. Create your "Shock and Awe" package and you will soon be playing in a field of 1 with ZERO competition. But you have to get all of this into your prospects hands **BEFORE YOU TALK TO THEM**, if at all possible.

This is all especially important for those remodeling businesses that are actually trying to grow and scale. Why? Because in most small businesses the owner/CEO is still the primary sale person and should be until they can hire a new sales person.

Building out a quality sales team is one of the hardest things to do in any business. It is insanely difficult to find one sales person as good as the original owner, and if you found 3 that were as good as you, you would be extremely lucky. Finding 10 or 20 A+ sales people is near impossible if you aren't delaying the sales process and getting high quality information to the prospect well before a selling conversation.

To grow and scale you have to make it easier on your sales team. You have to! You don't have a choice. You cannot just use brute force in your market to try and sell everyone you come in contact with. It does not work like that and never will. Improving your sales process actually starts with improving your marketing and overall positioning in your market.

You can hire all the sales trainers in the world to improve the sales people and sales process you have now and it can have an impact, but for how long and to what degree? Typically, people are who they are and can only marginally improve on their current skills so your selling system has to be damn good.

Instead look to integrate a marketing system that does most of the heavy lifting for you and your sales team. You must achieve a level of predetermination in the mind of the prospect to want what you have before you speak to them. It allows mediocre sales people to show up and WIN new sales without being an All Star.

Let's Look at These 2 Scenarios and You Will See Why "Delaying the Sale" Makes Perfect Sense:
Contractor A and **Contractor B** operate in the same city, let's say Boston. Both offer premium siding installation with typical jobs running around $20,000 per home.

Both have a solid team of installers and sales people.
Both market their businesses equally.
The term "contractor" isn't my favorite term to describe the profession but for this example it is what we are going to use.

Contractor A has a nice looking website and offers a "Free In-Home Estimate" as their only offer to learn more about them.

Contractor B has a small, but very focused website that is mobile responsive and offers a Free Guide called "The 7 Things You MUST Know Before Hiring a Siding Remodeler in Boston". She also offers a free in-home consultation, but the free guide is the most prominent offer on her site and displayed in all of her marketing. At this stage in the process, she only asks the prospect to give her their name and email address and in exchange, she sends them the free guide online.

Also, the guide is authored by her, has her picture on the cover, and a welcome letter that quickly builds "know, like, and trust". The prospect now knows the person behind this business.

Contractor A tries to educate the prospect by offering lots of content on their site in the form of blog posts, social media, and lots of web pages.

Contractor B gives her prospects exactly what they want to know and answers their 7 most pressing questions in a format that is easy to get, easy to read, easy to download, and explains in clear language the remodeling process and what the next steps should be.

She also offers a 2nd step in this process where she offers to send them (if they give her complete address details), in the mail, her "Home Exterior Transformation Kit" complete with a welcome letter, business card, most recent press release, her 7 Things guide, a cd, samples, and a catalog. She sends this in the mail within 24 hours and calls this her "shock and awe" package.

Contractor B also automatically sends out 12 emails over a 6 week period teaching the client more about their company, their philosophy, and providing as much value as she can to fully prepare the prospect to become a client. She has also clearly stated her Unique Selling Proposition and Guarantee throughout the guide and the email nurturing sequence further differentiating herself from the competition.

Contractor A collects their leads and passes them immediately on to a sales person who calls and tries to set an appointment. The prospect doesn't want to be sold yet but wasn't offered any other way to take the next step so they agree to the free estimate at their home the following week.

They meet at the home, the sales person hands them a business card, does a nice job of explaining the service and answering the prospects questions, and then prepares an estimate. This prospect will review the estimate in a day or two along with 2 or 3 additional quotes that they are gathering.

At this point, the prospect for Contractor A is either in or out. There really is no follow up and they have not established a clear differentiator. In the prospects mind, Contractor A is just another quote and appears mostly the same to the prospect. The sales person will follow up in a few days after sending out the estimate to see if they have been chosen to do the work.

Contractor B receives a call 4 weeks later from the same prospect that had read the guide, read some of the emails, and has received the kit in the mail. The prospect was really impressed with the level of knowledge and value she had provided and was ready to take the next step. The prospect felt a level of comfort with Contractor B vs. Contractor A. The prospect did not see the need to call 2 or 3 other remodelers at this point.

Her prospect had also received the "Home Exterior Transformation Kit" in the mail and was able to see and feel the level of detail and care that they put into this package; again, this is all before they ever spoke with a sales person. She had quickly built "know, like, and trust" with the prospect BEFORE THEY EVER SPOKE and had "showed up like no one else".

Hopefully this paints a clear picture of why this strategy is so important. And often times it does extend the sales cycle a bit but you will win a lot more deals by delaying the sale using better marketing to start. You will ATTRACT more leads and prospects to you by taking this approach and you will close more deals with a lot less resistance and at a higher price point.

Some of you won't like the idea of not pouncing on your prospects. You are used to going right for the kill and doing so very quickly. It feels good to win sales quickly but you will also lose more deals over the long haul if any of your competitors do all of the things outlined in a system like Lead Engine.

There is a lot more to this strategy than what is written on this page. I challenge you to take us up on our offer to do a 1 on 1 Consultation at www.PME360.com/invitation and we can help you figure out an initial plan of attack to double, or even triple your current remodeling business.

Strategy 1- Identify Yourself: Find, Seal and Deliver Your Niche

Focus and Find Your Niche vs Offering Everything

Part of developing a competition crushing online marketing strategy is all about getting enough of the right exposure in front of the right audience. If you are a remodeling business that offers a lot of services, you are in danger of failing to get the exposure you need to generate enough leads for each of your services.

Do you want to dominate your local market, make a lot of money and get more freedom with your remodeling business? Then why on earth are you offering so many remodeling services? If you have a large marketing budget and an incredible team, go for it, but most of you do not have these luxuries.
Please, please, please do not spread yourself too thin.

I know why you do spread yourself thin. I did the same thing when I started out in the remodeling and home building industry. I felt that I needed to offer everything and be everything to everyone to pay the bills. I was developing sub-divisions, building custom homes, build spec homes, putting up additions, remodeling bathrooms, taking a siding job, etc. It was madness! I would ask myself…."How can I refuse a $15,000 deck addition? The person is right here and wants me to do this. I cannot say no - can I?"

It's hard to say NO when you know you can do the work. But if you know it's not what you are the best in the world at doing, then why do it at all? Offering a full suite of remodeling services is extremely hard to manage and dangerous not only for your business, but for your reputation and long term business goals.

Google Loves Simplicity

A massively important thing to remember about dominating your local market online is that search engines like Google love simplicity. Google is, after all, just a giant computer trying to make sense and organize every single page of information on the web. And if you can make your messaging, service, and product consistent and easy to understand, you stand a much better chance of ranking, getting quality traffic, and attracting a higher quality prospect. If you are confusing yourself, odds are you are probably confusing the search engines and better yet, your prospects.

Remember, your prospects want to work with specialists NOT generalists and they are willing to pay more for a higher level of expertise whether its real or perceived.

Let's look at the concept of "theming" and focusing on one remodeling niche, and how it relates to marketing a remodeling niche versus doing everything as a general remodeler.

General Remodeling "Biz A"
Vs
Roofing Remodeler "Biz B"

Biz A has about 30 pages of content on their site. They have done a good job at optimizing for keywords + the local area they serve. But here is what Google sees:

- General Remodeling Overview
- General About Us
- Service 1 + Area
- Service 2 + Area
- Service 3 + Area
- Service 4 + Area
- Service 5 + Area
- Service 6 + Area
- Service 7 + Area
- Service 8 + Area
- Service 9 + Area
- Roofing Service 10 + Area
- General Remodeling Blog
- General Reviews/Testimonials

The search engines and your prospects understand that you are a remodeler, but nothing jumps out at them as something you are approaching an expert level status on. You can definitely rank for good keywords and get traffic and leads, but you will never beat "Biz B" at dominating the roofing market because here is what Google sees for them:

- Roofing Overview
- Roofing About Us
- Roofing Process
- Roofing History
- Roofing Products
- Roofing Service 1 + Area
- Roofing Service 2 + Area
- Roofing Service 3 + Area
- Roofing FAQ + Area
- Roofing Guarantee
- Roofing Blog
- Roofing Reviews
- Roofing Financing
- Roofing Videos
- Roofing Estimate (I prefer calling it a "Free 10 Point Roof Analysis + Estimate")

The idea is that it won't be very hard for Google to determine that the website is all about roofing. Everything that is said about this company online relates to roofing. It has a very specific "theme" It also won't be very hard for the prospect that is looking for a roofer + area they live, to pick Biz B to contact. Simple. Easy to understand and easy for prospects to determine what you are all about.

Personally, I have put together online marketing campaigns for both types of clients and both work to a certain degree. But nothing works as well as the "Biz B" example. Those that focus on doing one or two things extremely well tend to make a lot more money and crush the competition. Especially if you want to rank in local search. Google is looking for that theme to make the connection that "Biz B is located in this area and provides this very specific service."

You can theme a site around the term "remodeling" but it's pretty general. The traffic and eventual leads from this term won't be super targeted.

The Complexity of Offering Everything in Remodeling

If you are currently a full scale remodeler, someone who offers and does everything, your business is probably in danger. You probably aren't making enough money, you are working long hours, you are still heavily involved in every project, and your team is making lots of mistakes on the job. General remodeling is a tough game and creates a lot of issues for the owners and employees.

Sound about right? You tell yourself all the time, "I cannot give up the whole house remodels nor can I give up the kitchen remodels or the siding jobs!" Ok, so do not. But I can tell you that you will probably never generate the kind of money that you envisioned when you first got into this business. It's too complex of an industry to offer everything. I guarantee you are making a lot of mistakes and have no ability to get any kind of freedom in your business. Even those of you who just provide one or two services run into complexity in your business.

First, remodeling work is not easy to begin with. There is a lot to it, and every project is somewhat customized. I do not care if you are replacing a roof, or installing new windows, remodeling a basement, adding on a deck...every single job is a little different.

You are already in a business that is hard to scale, meaning it's difficult to create efficiencies in. You are a manufacturer with no assembly line. At times, it's like assembling a custom car in a driveway, piece by piece, with no protection from the elements, no instructions, and by the way, the person you are assembling this for changes their mind halfway through! It isn't easy, so stop making it harder than it already is.

Second, you need a lot of money to market a full scale remodeling company. With every service you offer, you are competing with the businesses that focus on doing one thing. And they will most likely be able to do that one thing way better than you.

Guess whose marketing dollars are going to go further and create more impact? The business that is focused and can dedicate all their effort to one area of remodeling. There are millions of dollars to be made every year in just about every corner of the country doing just one thing. But it's hard to draw that line in the sand and say "Enough! We are only doing this one thing, and the rest we are stopping today!"

Third, you need a great team to master and effectively deliver high quality results for each service that you offer. You need to build systems, checklists, and follow ups for every service. Some services are similar and can follow the same system, but projects like a basement remodel versus installing a new roof are very different and defy the conformity needed to scale.

Dividing up your team into "Kitchen Division" and "Exterior Division" is crucial, but again, to build this kind of team takes a lot of time and money. If you have the money and can build a great team, by all means, you can succeed at being a full scale remodeling provider. If not, you better quickly decide right now what you can do really well and start weeding out the rest of your service line. Just remember, every single division needs its own USP (Unique Selling Proposition) and Unique Guarantee. I cannot stress this enough, and I will get to this point next.

If you do not have a lot of capital, your cash flow is tight or non-existent, and you want more freedom and scalability in your remodeling business, find one thing you can do extraordinarily well and do that – and only that. You might have to expand your target radius a bit if you live in a sparsely populated area, but I would much rather see people do that than try to be everything to everyone.

Strategy #2- USP: Crush it with Uniqueness and Kill it with a Great Guarantee

Guess what? You are NOT a "remodeling contractor!" If that is all that you think you are, you should probably stop right here and do something else. You are so much more than that.

Think about it. Do not you do the following in some way for each one of your clients?

- Change their lives
- Help them live more comfortably
- Create their dream space
- Protect them from the elements
- Help them snag more free time and enjoy their lives
- Deliver services that are maintenance free which, in turn
  - Allows them to spend more time with family
  - Results in less time repairing and servicing their home
  - Liberates them from ever painting again
- Save them money (energy costs, maintenance costs, hiring the wrong contractor, etc.)
- Improve storage and help them get organized
- Simplify their lives
- Increase the resale value of their home
- Make their home more marketable

I do not want you to compete on price alone ever again. And if you can develop a great USP (Unique Sales Proposition) you won't have to. The power that a great USP will give you is incredible but takes a little bit of time and tweaking to get it right. You need to find that message that will make your prospects line up to hire you at whatever price YOU determine is fair (within reason).

Every single service you offer needs a USP and a Unique Guarantee. Again, some of your services may overlap if you are a full scale remodeler, but most of your services are much different animals so you cannot replicate them. This is much easier to do when you are the king/queen of your market with one service but it can be done with a full scale remodeling company...if you have the time and the money.

For instance, if I was developing a USP for a roofer in Denver, I might combine that with my Unique Guarantee (which we will talk about later) and create one power message.

"Providing Guaranteed Roofs for Life in Denver with Free Lifetime Repairs." Or *"We Shield You From the Elements in Denver, Guaranteed. Home of the Lifetime Roof and Free Lifetime Repairs."*

This was something I came up with in 5 seconds, but it says a lot if you read it closely. You are more than just a roofing company. You are the only company in Denver that provides a lifetime guarantee on your roof and free lifetime repairs to that roof you installed. You are also stating that you stand behind your product 100% and are so confident in it your service and product that you will show up and make any service repairs for the life of that roof. Powerful stuff!

If I was at a party and someone asked me what I did, I would not answer, *"I am a roofer."* I would repeat my power statement (USP) in some way, like *"I am the CEO of XYZ Roofing - we provide quality roofs in Denver with a 40 year guarantee and free lifetime repairs."* The person listening would remember you and what you did rather than the person who told them they were a just a another roofer or remodeler.

Who Would You Hire for Your Next Remodeling Project?

Who would you hire for your next roof remodel? The business that states *"we are a roofer in Denver"* or the business with the USP/Guarantee I created above? So many remodelers get this so wrong. As a result, they do not market themselves the right way because they have no message. Marketing extends beyond just your materials and ads.

Your messaging needs to encompass your entire company, even if you are a one-person shop. Make sure your marketing message is everywhere including your email signature, how you answer the phone, your business cards and even your return address labels.

Having the right guarantee and the right message makes your sales process a lot easier as well. Why? Because you have created an emotional reaction in your prospect in some way which is how they buy. This all starts with a power statement about your service.

You, or you sales people, can easily set yourself apart from the crowd when talking with any hot prospect by repeating your USP and Unique Guarantee. Try it out. Test a USP and Unique Guarantee on your next sales call and see how your prospect responds to it. If it is strong enough, there is probably no competition at that point and the decision will be much easier for them, even if you are more expensive than the next company.

Focus So You Can Grow

Creating the right strategy and marketing campaigns is extremely hard to do if you are offering too many services unless you have a large amount of capital to market each service, a great team that is highly skilled in all the areas you are offering, and you have the motor of the energizer bunny to keep everyone motivated and on task.

Do not get me wrong. I love working with big remodeling businesses that truly get how to completely dominate an entire market for all of the remodeling services they can get their hands on. But this is rare. Most of you need to focus and stop the insanity of doing too many things.

Last but not least, do you plan on selling your business at any point? If you are on the smaller side, you will never get anyone to buy what you have if you are too scattered. Selling a remodeling business is not easy but it can be done if you have a proven niche, turn-key systems, lead flow, revenue, and a business that crushes it. Keep it simple and I guarantee you will make way more money than those who insist on doing it all.

Building Your USP in Under an Hour

There are a lot of courses and books out there just on the topic of building a Unique Selling Proposition. I will hopefully reduce your learning curve so you can quickly (right after you read this book!) craft a USP that should beat most of your competition. In fact, most of them do not even have a USP so you will quickly become the king/queen of your market if you take the time to build one.

The most important question you need to ask yourself is "What is the #1 reason someone should hire me for their next remodeling project rather than my competition?" You need to be able to answer this question quickly and with confidence and elegance.

If your first response is "quality" or "craftsmanship", that isn't going to cut it. That is the kind of answer that your competitor who went out of business last month used on every sales call. Everyone says that. You need to be better than that and can begin by crafting a marketing message with a unique angle. Apply the two-part USP to your business by thoughtfully answering the following questions:

- ✓ What is it that you do that is unique?
- ✓ What can you guarantee that is special?

With these answers beginning to rumble around in your mind, you can create a powerful USP in under an hour by following these three steps:

- Create an Emotional Connection with Your Prospect
- Define your Target Client
- Decide What You Stand for and Make it a Unique Guarantee

Step 1 – Create an Emotional Connection with Your Prospect

This step isn't typically covered in building a USP but I feel that you cannot build a one without creating an emotional connection with your prospect and target audience.

You have to tell your story to the world even if you feel it's a boring one, which I bet it's not. Everyone has a story to tell but remodeling contractors completely miss this. Building a corporate brand takes ten times as long as building a personal brand. Why?

People do not connect emotionally to brands the way that they do to people.

Look at the explosive popularity of reality TV shows against the decline of well-acted sitcoms. People love other people's stories. If you can get your story out there, your history, accomplishments, your failures, and tell the world who you are as a person and founder of this business, you will succeed faster!

Everyone loves to see the underdog succeed. If your prospects see that you overcame great obstacles to get to where you are they can relate to you and just might want to buy from you because of it. Business *is* personal, and people buy from other *people.*

Creating your emotional connection is probably going to come from creating a great About Us, History page, FAQ section, and Guarantee page and sprinkling your story throughout your entire site. (By the way - Every website should have the pages I just listed on their website.) Make sure you also have your photo, bios and your entire team distributed throughout as well.

Your Prospects are Terrified of Making the Wrong Choice

Your sleazy competition is making it hard on you. How? By not showing up for work, by disappearing with initial deposits, by doing shoddy work and not standing behind it, by using subpar materials and craftsmanship to up their profit...the list goes on.

This is the most overlooked piece of marketing a remodeling business. Stop telling everyone how great you are and start answering the questions that actually concern every prospect. Every single prospect of yours is TERRIFIED of hiring you and making the wrong decision. Sympathize with them. Let them know you understand their fears and concerns. Put it all on the table.

Develop an FAQ section that puts all the negative stuff they are thinking about out in the open. Think about everything your prospect is scared of happening and have a great response for it.

Here are some typical concerns most of your prospects have:

- If you replace my roof, will there be nails all over my yard?

- I just replaced my hardwood floors and now I want my windows replaced. Are you going to ruin my new floors when replacing my windows?
- Are you insured? What happens if one of your employees gets injured at my home?
- What happens if one of your employees gets injured at my home?
- Do you use sub-contractors or employees?
- Are any of your employees or contractors ex-convicts?
- Who is going to be in my home when I am not there?
- Where will your crew go to the bathroom?
- Will they be required to wear shirts on the job?
- What kind of guarantee do you have if I am not happy?
- How much am I going to have to put down as a deposit to get started?
- Do you offer financing?
- Do you offer payment plans?
- Does your crew wear belts? No seriously. I do not want to see any "plumber crack."

I could go on for hours with lists of questions that your best prospects are thinking about and concerned with and even fearful of. Sit down with your team or your spouse, partner, friend, etc. and start brainstorming a list of questions your prospects would ask.

And here is a final tip on this - do not be afraid to make it funny. Again, you are trying to develop an emotional connection here and humor is rarely found in the remodeling market. The one above about the belt wearing is one example, or the shirts, or the bathroom. You can make that funny and also stop their fears at the same time. Differentiate yourself from everyone else as much as possible and build that strong emotional connection.

Step 2 – Define Your Target Client

I do not like the term customer. I think it's outdated. I much prefer client. I would much rather be referred to as a remodeling client than a customer. This is something to think about when developing your marketing message.

Who is your target client?

- Demographically?
- Do you have a specific niche?
    - Residential vs Commercial
    - Specific Service
- What specific problem do you solve?

For this example, I am going to continue with my Denver Roofer.

- My target demographic is:
    - Homeowners
    - Middle Class Earning $60,000 - $80,000 Per Year
    - Women vs Men? Who is making the buying decision? (Males and females tend to gravitate toward and decide on specific remodeling services.)
    - Location – Denver, CO area
- Niche
    - Residential Roofs
    - Do I offer any differentiators?
        - How do I dispose of the previous roof? Recycle it?
        - Materials I use are free of harmful ___?
        - Keeps your home cooler in the heat?
- Problem
    - Keep my clients homes dry and safe from the elements
    - Keep out the elements
    - Protect their most precious asset, their family, from the harsh Denver climate

Step 3 – Decide What You Stand for and Make it a Unique Guarantee

To develop a killer USP you have to stand for something. What do you stand behind and for how long? Why?

This will go hand in hand with your Unique Guarantee and can easily be incorporated into your USP. Think about you, your remodeling service, your demographic target, your personality, and the products you are using. I bet you can easily incorporate the manufacturer's warranty into your Unique Guarantee along with your own extended service backing.

You have to take into account your unique life experience and the emotional connection you are trying to build. For example:

"I am offering this 100-year guarantee because I have been burned in the past by contractors who do not do things the right way. I believe so much in my product and service that I will go to the ends of the earth, or in this case, back to your home to make sure you are happy. Our services aren't the least expensive, but they are the best and that's what is important to most people. Getting the job done once the right way and having a company stand behind it."

Make this personal because it is personal. After all, your remodeling company probably has your name on it.

Some questions to answer about you and your product:

- How long can you service the product and stand behind the service? I bet you it's longer than you think if you install the product correctly.
- How much does it cost you to service your service/product?
- Can you build this into your price?

Creating a Unique Promise and a Compelling Offer

Now, ask yourself some additional questions:
- Can I offer a unique price, financing, or payment plan option?
- Do I have a level of care or customized touch that no one else has?
- Do I have a delivered benefit(s) from the service that can be quantified?
- Do I have quality that is unheard of in my marketplace?
- Do I have a unique experience that has led me to deliver my service in a certain way?

Time Frame
- How long will it take you to finish your work?
- Can you guarantee that the work will be done by X number of days or else (what)?

What Happens If You Do not Deliver On Your Promise?

- Will you provide cash back or additional services if you do not deliver on time? Or if you make a mistake?
- "We will get your roof replaced and installed in under 14 days, or else we will pay you $100 cash each day that the project isn't completed after the two week period."
- "We will give you $50 cash for each (nail, shingle, debris) you find in your yard or home."

Final Notes:

Your USP should be anywhere from 1 to 10 sentences and again, you should build one for every service you offer. You can slice and dice it up for various purposes. Everyone in your organization needs to have this in front of them at all times and have it memorized. If you get this right, everything else that follows will be much easier.

Strategy 3 - Content: If the Prince had Good Content, He Would be King

A lot has been said everywhere about internet content. It can be a complicated topic if you let it. As suggested before it's all about keeping it simple and keeping the following three content concepts in mind:

- Print Readers Read, Web Readers Scan
- The average time spent on a webpage is about 25 seconds
- 72% of business website owners do not address benefits

This means the following:

- **Use benefits instead of features**

  <u>Feature:</u> We use weather resistant siding that resists the elements.

  <u>Benefit:</u> You'll never have to paint your house again!

- **Use one idea per sentence**

  <u>For example, this sentence has three ideas:</u>
  As a local custom homebuilder with over thirty years of industry experience, we will make sure the job is done to your complete satisfaction.

  <u>Here is how that might be rewritten:</u>
  We are a local company to your area. Our team has over thirty years of homebuilding experience. Your satisfaction with our work is guaranteed.

- **Write in short sentences (7 to 15 words) and short paragraphs (3 to 5 sentences)**

  <u>For example, this sentence reads:</u>
  In addition to building custom homes, Joe Remodeler offers the following services: siding and roofing, additions, garages, kitchen and bathroom remodels, basement refinishes and more.

It might read better like this:

In addition to building custom homes, Joe Remodeler is able to complete other remodeling projects. If you are looking to update your home's exterior, we can provide siding and roofing solutions. For clients looking to expand their living space, we offer garages, additions and basement refinishing options. The Joe Remodeler team also specializes in kitchen and bathroom remodeling.

- **Address the website to your client or prospect. Use** *You* **as much as possible, instead of** *We, Us or I.*

Website Viewing

There have been studies on the way people view websites—what draws them in:

- **F-pattern:** Studies tracking eyeball movements on computer screens suggest that viewers read websites using an F pattern eye scan (see example below).
- **Webpage Position:** Content placed in premium positions on the page is perceived as more important.
- **Bolding: Bolded** type attracts the eye because of the contrast with the words around them.
- **Reading:** Figure that only 20% of the words on your page will be read.
- **Links:** The most used feature on a website page is links within the content.
- **Space**: Things in space stand out and are easier to distinguish.
- **Font:** Times New Roman is an example of serif font (thought to be better for print material); Verdana is an example of a sans serif font (thought to be better for screen reading)
- **Develop an easy-to-navigate website with a call to action** - and I mean easy. You have about four seconds to grab attention.
- **Lead them to the conversion**. Provide rich, changing and relevant content on the site - No bias, no bull content is what they are after.
- **Stay away from Flash** – Visitors will get distracted.
- **Avoid long uploads** – No one will stick around for them.

- **Display a commitment to social issues** - If you're involved in environmental friendly remodeling, show it on your site. It will leave a favorable impression.
- **Produce customizable products and services** - Consumers want the remodeling geared to them. Make it about them, not you!
- **Know your company** - Consumers want to read company mission and vision statements and know you're ethical.
- **Add Proof Elements –** Proof elements like review site logos and linking to your latest reviews are crucial to have "above the fold" on your site. If you have been featured in any newspapers, local shopping magazines or even national websites and magazines, make sure you feature those on your site for the world to see. The reasons are obvious!

How people view websites

Eyetracking Study (F-Pattern)[5]

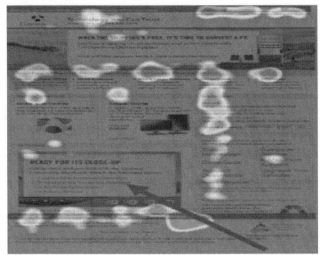

Home Page- Notice how the images are not viewed. (This is called banner blindness.)

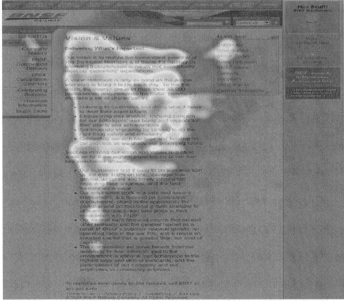

About Us Page- Reading in an F pattern

You can see how important content is for the internet viewer. If you're not comfortable with writing it yourself, you might consider hiring an internet copywriter like the team at PME 360 to get it right for you.

Strategy #4 – Local Search: Discover How Important a "NAP" Really Is

The Local Search Ecosystem

Without getting into too much detail about how the Local Search Ecosystem works exactly, the complexity of local search is significant. It also changes often so it takes some time to get up to speed and stay current on how exactly to get your local business to rank in local search.

The Local Search Ecosystem is made up of local directories, social sites, yellow books, vertical directories, daily deal sites, geo (geographic) directories, map sites, and review sites. Every single one of these sites could be important to your business. Your prospects in your local market are on these sites. If you aren't on there, you do not exist in their eyes, or you may force your prospects to start asking questions about the validity of your business.

You cannot do Reputation Marketing **(Strategy #6)** as a local business without incorporating local search. Let's talk a little bit more about why managing your reputation online is important with local listings.

> ➢ According to Myles Anderson of Bright Local, *"Having your correct business details widely available is positive for local SEO and sets you up nicely to take advantage of the mobile-boom."*[6]

> ➢ Similarly, Wiley Cerilli, Vice-President and General Manager of SinglePlatform notes that

> *"Consumers are using the internet as a discovery engine and the opportunity for a local business to be found by their next great customer continues to grow. It is important for small businesses to list their products, services, and menus across the sites that consumers use to make their purchasing decisions.*

> *Equally important in today's mobile world is making sure your online content like websites and digital storefronts can be viewed on mobile devices. As smartphone adoption continues to rise, being a mobile-*

friendly business is becoming a necessity."[7]

Want to Rank in Google Places and Google Maps?

Detailed and correct local listings also make it easy for Google to find, recognize and rank your local business in Google maps and Google places. This is the primary method they are using to rank local businesses in their Google Places for Business. 90% of the remodeling businesses I look at have not claimed their Google Places account, and the ones that have are doing it all wrong.

Furthermore, since Google has said in the past that roughly 20 percent of PC-based search and 40-50 percent of mobile search is related to location and local information, it is important to claim, update, and enhance online information about your business immediately, or struggle to be found in search results.

Many local businesses still do not realize that they need to claim and optimize all the local listings that their business is entitled to on sites like:

- Google Places (www.google.com/placesforbusiness/)
- Yelp (http://www.yelp.com/)
- Yahoo (http://local.yahoo.com/)
- Bing Local (www.bing.com/local/us/)

Business owners can control these listings, as they are often free to set up, or may already exist and need to be claimed.

Local Business Listing Survey Results

Constant Contact's Single Platform Division has released the results of a new SMB survey which polled more than 350 SMBs.[8] This survey bolsters Search Engine Land's assertion that most small businesses are overwhelmed and confused by even basic online marketing, as reflected in some of the following contradictory findings:

- 49 percent say they've never updated their listings online.
- 50 percent have seen listings for their business that are not accurate.
- 70 percent say they do not have the time to manage listings on all of the sites that consumers use.

- Only 23 percent have a good sense of how listings drive traffic to their business.
- 85 percent said it's important for them to be found on major search sites, local search, apps and directory sites.
- 78 percent believe that new customers will find them through these sites and apps.

The major takeaway from these findings is that while business owners have some sense of the value of local business listings, they either do not have the time or the know-how to attack this challenge.

You may or may NOT have a website. At this point it doesn't really matter. This strategy can work **with or without** a website so do not stress. Ideally, any local business that is serious about growing and dominating their local market should at least have a nice one to three page website that they can drive traffic to, but it is not a requirement for this to work.

You can try this out right now by doing a search for your company name on Google.

- What would a prospect see?
- Is there enough good information about your business to have the prospect want to take the next steps?
- Is your business information appearing correctly in the search results?
- Does your company look like it could be out of business?
- Are competitors listed on page one for your company name?
- Could doubt about the validity of your business creep into the prospect's mind?

You should be dominating page 1-3 of Google, Yahoo, and Bing for your business name. You should have lots of different search results appearing... from local listings, updated social profiles, vertical directories, good content, quality reviews (that are user generated) and your website should be appearing (if you have one).

And one more thing that I haven't mentioned that may be important to your business. All things being equal, those local businesses that have consistent and more local listings than their competitors, outrank their competitors on Google for competitive local terms more often than not. What would that mean to your local business to outrank them in Google for key terms related to your services?

Get Your NAP Right

Before you take on the task of listing your business in every directory you can find, the absolute first step is to determine what you intend to use for your local business information. This is your NAP (**N**ame, **A**ddress and **P**hone) and should be used the exact same way in every local listing. You cannot rank in local search without a consistent NAP online. And you want lots of quality websites, especially local listing directories, to display your NAP exactly as you have determined it should be shown.

Name - How do you write your business name? If we sometimes filled out directory listings as "PME 360 Inc." and sometimes as "PME 360," we would have some issues with the accuracy of our local business information. Do not complicate things. Use one name clearly across the board and become that brand, and only that brand.

Consider finding out how Google currently lists your business address and use that as your model. Search for your business name online and see if Google currently sees you as "XYZ Remodeling, Inc." or "XYZ Remodeling." If Google sees your business name a certain way, it's probably for a reason and you might want to move forward with using that as your brand name everywhere online including your website. You don't have to do it this way, but if Google sees your brand name a certain way, it is probably not by accident.

Address - Decide how you are going to write your address. Will you use "St." or spell out "Street"? This may sound particular but your address display needs to be consistent. Find out how Google currently lists your business address and use that as your model. If Google currently sees you at "5700 South Lake Shore Drive" and you feel that you can live with that, use that everywhere online including your website.

Phone - This seems easy enough but some local business listings require a local phone number rather than an 800 number. If you use tracking numbers for your business you want to make sure that you choose one main number to use for your local business information.

What if I Do Not Have an Office?

Google Places currently requires that you have a physical address to use for your listing – not a P.O. box. There is hope that this rule will be amended by Google, as many contractors work our of their homes and do not have a physical business address, per se. If you find yourself in this predicament, there are a few options:

1. Use your home address. If you are comfortable disclosing your home address, this is often the easiest way to get around the P.O. Box rule.

2. Use a personal mailbox (PMB). Some companies provide mailboxes and mail services through their storefront (The UPS Store, Mailboxes Unlimited). Your address will include a physical location plus a PMB number.

3. Partner with another provider. If you have a colleague (not someone who is direct competition) that has a physical location, you may consider using their address with their permission. This is the least desirable option, because if they go out of business or move locations, you will be back to square one.

Citations are Vital

Citations are your NAP written out on a webpage (local directory, social site, review site, vertical directory, etc.) other than your own. These may or may not include a link to your website. If you have a website and can get a link back to your site, these citations also become powerful link building strategies.
The more times you have proper and consistent citations throughout the web, the more likely you are to appear in search and local search sites:

- This leads to more traffic and leads for your business.
- It reduces market confusion.
- Your business name dominates when people are researching your business.

All other factors being equal, businesses with a greater number of citations will probably rank higher than competitors businesses with fewer citations. If you do not have enough citations that are done correctly, you will not outrank your competitors in local search.

How to Do Your Citations Properly

Establish a consistent NAP that you will use to represent your business. Be consistent and accurate.

Identify the top 100 local directories and local business review sites and start verifying your listing. If no listing appears for your business yet, set one up. Once you have mastered the top 100 directories, start looking for vertical directories (directories specific to your business, Google "your business type + directory"). There are hundreds of thousands of these out there. Add as many as you can each month that are relevant and of good quality.

Rinse and repeat! Unfortunately, this is an ongoing process and needs to be managed monthly. The more listings you get, the more traffic and leads you will get. There is no tool that can do this for you. It requires good old fashion manual labor. (You can also outsource this to a reputable local search marketing agency.)

Local Content

When you hear the term local content, it is referring to:

- Directions to individual locations
- Reviews (user generated)
- Bios
- Talk about the location
- Built in individual landing pages (huge)
- Local guest blogging opportunities
- Videos
- Articles

Google's steadily growing focus on local internet search should have small business owners very excited about the future of their online marketing endeavors. It looks like Google will increasingly tailor its search services to reward small businesses that take the right steps to market to their local community.

This means that people looking online for products, services, answers, and more, will receive local search results that better fit their needs. They also will be more likely to find your business!

Geographically Targeted Landing Pages (also known as geo-targeted, locally targeted pages, mini-sites or local landing pages)

The goal for this local search strategy is to build out lots of "Service + City" or "Service + State" landing pages to drive local traffic in those markets. Think of all the possible "local" terms that are used to describe a region:

- Surrounding cities and towns
- Counties
- States
- Neighborhoods
- Zip Codes

You can use all of these to build out separate pages for each of them. Examples might be Gold Coast, or the Magnificent Mile in Chicago which can refer to the same area.

If you belong to any industry (like the National Association of The Remodeling Industry) or local business (Palatine Chamber of Commerce) associations, you should place these "authority links" on your landing page and link out to those associations in a new window. Do the same with review sites like Yelp! and Google +.

Pull in the Google map of your office location and create original content for each geo-targeted landing page. You can reword it from pages you already have such as those on your main website. Pull in other content like images, video, reviews, association links, etc. and you should have a great chance of ranking.

You want to be careful with this strategy as you do not want to build low quality pages with little content or duplicate content on them. With the Google Panda updates, low quality content pages and duplicate content pages can get your entire domain penalized. If you build out geo-targeted pages make them great with at least 500 words and good local unique content.

The Importance of Local Search

With an ever increasing set of options out there, consumers are seeking more comprehensive business information. According to piece in *Search Engine Land*, this should include "basic information, more personalized information (directions to the business from a user's location), and dynamic information that changes regularly, including product availability, prices, deals, and more."[9]

Businesses that provide more information will stand a better chance at winning the local internet search game.

Finally, keep in mind this comment from Ed Parsons, the Geospatial Technologist of Google, from a recent talk at Google PinPoint on how prevalent local search is today: *"About one in three queries that people just type into a standard Google search bar are about places, they are about finding out information about locations. This isn't Google Maps, just people normally looking at Google."*[10]

Strategy #5 SEO: Organic and Paid SEO Can Change Your Life

You have probably heard of SEO. It may seem like a concept that's shrouded in techno-land but it really is pretty simple. The term means Search Engine Optimization. It is simply the process of making visible a website or a web page in a search engine's organic (natural or unpaid) search on the Search Engine Results Page (SERP).

The idea is to have your remodeling site appear on page one – and rank #1-3 if you can – of the SERP or as close to it as possible. This is partly done through a combination of good quality content and meta tags (a descriptive HTML tag which provides keywords and summarizes content). But is all starts with keywords and good content and incorporating some of the strategies from the previous chapter.

Keywords

Keywords are what people use to search for your business. For example, if you're a "remodeler in Memphis", that's a keyword. Potential clients might search for you like that. The latest thinking is to create keywords with a tail (called long tail keywords) and keep them local, if possible (A remodeler in the Germantown area, for example). You can even throw in a ZIP code, county, neighborhood, or state if that's the best way to capture local search traffic.

To start, you need to know what keywords are being searched in your local market. To see if they're being used by others, there are free and paid tools on the internet that will let you know the number of monthly searches by keyword. The results on the following page are from the free Google AdWords tool (adwords.google.com/o/KeywordTool) after plugging in "Remodeler in Memphis."

Keyword	Competition	Global Monthly Searches ?	Local Monthly Searches ?
remodeler in memphis ▾	·	·	·

⊟	✓ Save all	**Keyword ideas (100)**		1 - 50 of 100 ▾	‹	›

Keyword	Competition	Global Monthly Searches ?	Local Monthly Searches ?
bathroom remodeling memphis tn ▾	High	140	140
kitchen remodeling memphis ▾	High	170	170
home remodeling memphis tn ▾	High	91	91
memphis bathroom remodeling ▾	High	260	210
memphis home remodeling ▾	High	210	210
memphis yellow pages ▾	Medium	2,400	2,400
memphis directions ▾	Low	3,600	2,900
yellow pages memphis ▾	Medium	2,400	2,400
home remodeling ideas ▾	High	9,900	6,600
memphis home ▾	Medium	60,500	49,500
home remodeling contractors ▾	High	14,800	14,800
memphis tennessee remodeling ▾	High	390	390
remodeling ideas ▾	High	90,500	74,000
what to do in memphis ▾	Low	27,100	22,200

As you can see, the search term "remodeler in Memphis" is not producing any results that are being tracked by Google. But, Google will start spitting out a bunch of related phrases that might be more specific and related to your business. If you aren't getting any results you might be searching for keywords that are too specific and that no one ever searches for.

Try taking a step back and finding some more general keywords. Check out what people search for in your industry. (Example: try the keyword "remodeling" vs "remodeler" and see what people search for more frequently across the globe.) Now go back and try geo-modifying the best term with your zip code, county, state, neighborhood, etc. There is a ton of low competition, high converting local keywords that are being searched in every corner of this earth that your competitors haven't thought about. Put yourself in the mind of your top prospects and think of all the ways they might search online to find a business like yours.

Do not be afraid of competition levels at this point. It might be easier to rank for those terms than you think especially if you have a domain that includes some of the words you are trying to rank for (ex: www.ABCMemphisRemodeling.com or www.ABCMemphisRoofing.com).

There are very few remodeling companies that do everything right when it comes to online marketing and if you can do most of what I mention in this book fairly well you should dominate. There isn't a local market on earth that I haven't been able to achieve awesome results for online. If you work at it and apply the steps in this book you will rank, you will get traffic, and you will get high quality leads.

Keep keywords closely related to your business. In other words, if you are a roofer in Atlanta, do not use The Atlanta Falcons as a keyword just because it gets a lot of searches.

Website Search Engine Optimization

You do not see meta tags on your website. They are placed behind the scenes by your web developer. They consist of:

- Meta Title: 60 to 70 characters
- Meta Description: 150 to 200 characters

You can discover what your competitors are using for meta tags by doing the following:

- Move your cursor to go to the right of the home webpage
- Right click
- Click on view source

This is what you will see (This example is from a siding contractor in Chicago):

```
<title>Chicago Siding Contractor</title>
<META NAME="Keywords" CONTENT="chicago siding contractor">
<META NAME="Description" CONTENT="Siding can be a worthwhile investment that can pay off with the right siding contractor. As
your Chicago Siding Contractor we understand this.">
```

Seeing the tags of a competitor might help you to determine the best ones for your website. Make sure that you use the keywords and the meta tags in coherent ways in the content on your page. It's best that you write different tags for each page of your site. However, if you do nothing else, make sure they are on your homepage.

Your two key tags should contain the following:

- **Title Tag:** List the Service + Location + Zip Code of what you are trying to get traffic for (60 characters).
- **Meta Description:** Describe the page in a well-written 160 character meta description. Include your service, location, and zip code.

Other tags, called headline or heading tags (H1, H2, H3, etc.) should also contain local search information such as:

- Hire a Roofing Contractor in Schaumburg Today
- Get a Free Siding Estimate in Portland Today
- See What Our Memphis, TN Siding Installation Clients Say About Us (and give a real testimonial or repost a review here...it's an easy way to get more local authoritative content in your site!)

Combining Content and SEO

Below is the homepage of the same Chicago Siding Contractor website. Notice that all of the meta tags and keywords are used in the content. This is important for search engines. When they "crawl" the internet in response to a search request, this is what they look for.

Meta tags

```
<title>Chicago Siding Contractor</title>
<META NAME="Keywords" CONTENT="chicago siding contractor">
<META NAME="Description" CONTENT="Siding can be a worthwhile investment that can pay off with the right siding contractor. As your Chicago Siding Contractor we understand this.">
```

Home Page

Sleet, snow, rain, hail, frost, heat and humidity - Chicago can be an extreme environment for your house. Your siding has to be versatile enough to perform in all types of weather. The elements can take a beating on your home?s exterior and siding is critical in ensuring your investment and the safety and health of your family. As your **Chicago Siding Contractor** we understand this.

Siding is like the skin of you home and has two main functions, aesthetic and protective. A home with properly installed siding and insulation can save you hundreds of dollars a year on heating and cooling costs. Siding is the first thing people see when looking at your house and curb appeal is very important when showing your home to prospective buyers. New siding may also help you increase the value of your home and even sell it quicker. Siding can be a worthwhile investment **that can pay off** with the right siding contractor. It will protect what? s inside and give your home a beautiful exterior finish. It?ll be like having a new home.

Again, you can see that all of the meta tags have been used in the content. This is the best and easiest way to optimize your website for search engines. Do not try to do too much with each page. Have a plan and a keyword phrase or two that you want to focus on for that page and stop there. Develop more pages for other keywords you want to target.

Other SEO Practices

In addition to the basic organic SEO discussed above, there are other ways to optimize the content of your site to achieve higher positioning on the SERP. The basic idea of more sophisticated SEO is to get links back to your website. This means whenever you submit something about your business anywhere online, make sure you link back to your website if you can. That can be as simple as highlighting the words or phrase you want to use and linking it back to your site. (Do not overdo this! or you may get penalized by Google.)

For most remodeling businesses focus on getting your links from social signals (Facebook, Twitter, and Review Sites like Yelp and Google +), local listings, and targeted industry directories. Introducing guest blogging, content marketing, social bookmarking, and press releases are also a good strategy but can be time consuming. Also, you want to make sure you do not get to spammy with this.

The more you get your brand out there, the more visible your business will become:

- Sign up for a Facebook page.
- Sign up for a Twitter Account.
- Sign up on Google +.
- Create a LinkedIn Profile.
- Sign up for Google alerts to keep current with trends in your business.
- Sign up for a KnowEm account.

- Set up an account and bookmark your site on Delicious, Reddit and Digg.
- Especially with a brick and mortar business, sign up on every local directory possible.
- Submit your site to GoGuides.org, JoeAnt.com, Gimpsy.com, Business.com, Best of the Web and Manta.
- Engage in relevant online industry forums and back link to your sites.
- Become a guest blogger on My Blog Guest and other guest blogging sites.
- Write and submit pieces to EzineArticles, GoArticles, Articlesbase, Article Dashboard, IdeaMarketers, Article City or Article Alley.
- Submit a press release to either a free or paid distribution sites. Press releases announce news and can often lead to stories in newspapers or other publications.

Social Media Marketing and its Role in Organic/Local Search

You will notice that I have not written much in this book about social media marketing. An entire book could be written on this topic and a lot of social media marketing books exist. Let me give you a quick overview of what I think about social media. I am not a huge fan of social media as a direct driver of new business. Listen closely, social media will NOT directly drive you much, if any, new business.

"About 61% of small businesses do not see any return on investment on their social-media activities, according to a survey released Tuesday from Manta, a social network for small businesses. Yet, almost 50% say they've increased their time spent on social media, and only 7% have decreased their time."[11]

Local remodeling businesses waste a lot of time with social media and get very little direct return from it. Remodeling businesses should not invest a ton of time and money in social media (video and reviews excluded!). Being in the internet marketing world I realize that this is a bit contradictory, but I have seen far too many businesses get burned spending a ton of money on social media marketing and get ZERO return from it.

Investing some time and money into a few key areas of social media are well worth it, and for a few very important reasons. Below is a list of reasons you should do some social media and what to focus on:

1) **Your prospects expect you to be there:** Most of you have setup a Facebook Fan Page or Twitter page and even dabbled in YouTube. Great! If you have profiles set up, make sure you have stuff on them.

2) **Your prospects expect your social profiles to be updated:** Most prospects do not expect that you will be posting to your social profiles every day, but alarms are raised when the last social post on your Facebook page was from 2011. Do not let your social profiles become a ghost town, this is an easy way to lose credibility in your market and lose interested prospects. Feed your blog posts to your social profiles, videos, and other industry leading content.

3) **You need the signals:** No one knows for sure how much weight is put on social signals (posts, shares, visits, etc.) from your social media profiles and how this affects your ranking in local and organic search. We do know it does play a role and we do believe it will become more and more important as other means of generating links go away. At the very least, get some regular social signals to your profiles to help you rank in search.

4) **Focus on video:** For service based businesses like remodeling companies, video is going to be your best way to generate social signals, interest, and crush your competition. Every key member of your team should be equipped with a smart phone and be shooting exit interviews with each client.

   Get that video/exit interview posted as a testimonial on YouTube and some of the other top video sites. Not only will you have great visual content that confirms you are the best company to hire, but if done properly, you will get high quality links and a citation for your business online. Also, consider doing a 10-Step or 5-Step tutorial or discovery series about what makes your service unique. Shoot some real world examples of issues you run into with homes and explain how you resolve these situations.

5) **Focus on images:** Showcasing your best work and current projects on photo sharing sites like Flickr, Slideshare, Houzz, Google +, Facebook,

Instagram, Pinterest, etc can help your business get more traffic and help close more deals. Optimize each photo name, description, tags, and author for keywords, business name (NAP), and as much information as you can. Most of these social/photo sharing sites allow for easy embedding into your website which gives you some nice social signals and a great visual presentation for your prospects.

6) **Focus on blogging:** Blogging is a great way to get new content on your site. Search engines love sites that are updated regularly and having new blog content with an RSS Feed (Really Simple Syndication) is an easy way to accomplish that. Consider mixing in local content and current events in your market with content related to the service you are selling. This is probably going to be the best way for you to get additional social signals on Facebook, Twitter, and Google + by sharing your latest posts.

7) **Get a Reputation:** This really should be #1 on this list and I cover this in great detail in our next "Reputation Marketing" chapter. Yelp and Google + are definitely considered "social sites" along with most of the other top review sites. Focus on getting high quality reviews and sharing those reviews via your social profiles like Facebook and Twitter. This creates a double whammy effect and some good social signals and social links. This type of content has way more impact than trying to come up with something clever to post and share.

You do need to be doing social media just not the way you thought you did. It will help everything else you are trying to accomplish online and offline if you do have some good information in your social profiles.

Make sure you keep your profiles updated on a regular basis and that you consistently feed them. Do not let your profiles become dormant for too long or you will put doubt in the minds of your prospects about whether or not you are still in business. It seems crazy that something like this can turn an interested prospect off, but it does. So, **do not open a social account unless you are going to do something with it**. Just do not expect that you will drive a direct lead from this type of marketing, it just doesn't happen that way. Be extremely wary of any companies that claim you **need** to be on social media to directly drive new business.

Google AdWords Pay per Click (PPC) Basics

Around the year 2000, Google started paid search marketing with the idea of providing a targeted, yet simple solution for small businesses who wanted a cost effective way to advertise online. I guess you can throw in the Microsoft Adcenter paid search program as well into this discussion, it's at least worth trying to see if you can get some low cost traffic and leads.

The nice thing about paid search is you only pay when a prospect clicks on your ad and is sent to your website or landing page. It's a great way to get some quality local impressions (exposure) for your business, especially for those keywords that you do not show up for organically or in local search.

Some experts believe that paid search is going to go away soon, but I just do not think that is going to happen. Paid search is still a great way to get quality impressions (marketing is all about getting enough of the right impressions) for very specific keywords in your local market.

The idea is this:

Set a Business Objective: Typically, this is a certain action you want a prospect to take. That action could be to fill out a form, call for a free consultation, buy merchandise, sign up for a newsletter, etc. For paid search to work, you really need a very specific keyword to align with a very specific page and offer. Do not send your paid search traffic to your home page. Sending all your paid search traffic to your home page is a great way to blow through your paid search budget.

Select keywords: You want to use a keyword or phrase that a prospect will search with to find the website or landing page of your remodeling business. Since you have to pay for each click, select "buying keywords" to attract prospects who will get you to your goal. The rule of thumb is that the more specific a keyword phrase is, the more likely those who click on it will take some sort of action. Try including some misspellings, related searches, and even your top competitors names (as long as the business name is not trademarked) for keywords in your campaigns.

Set the match modifiers: You decide how close you want your keyword string to match the query of the searcher. For instance, your keyword might be "roofing remodeler." If you use a broad match (this is the default match), your ad may appear at any time when someone searches for roofing remodeler. If you decide on a narrower match, your ad will not be displayed as often. A narrower match might be "roofing modeler in the Chicagoland area." I highly recommend using all four match types including negative matches.

Place your bid: The AdWords platform is set up as an auction. The best placement on the page goes to the highest bidder after a check for relevance and quality. You can establish your spend for each day and even for each visitor. You can also schedule your ads to run at certain times of the day. You can set some pretty sophisticated bids, but as a general rule of thumb consider investing more in your [Exact Match] keywords followed by "Phrase Match" and finally broad match. Broad match keywords are typically worth the least to your campaign so do not over spend on these.

Create your ad: Google dictates character counts (25 to 30) for each line of the ad which includes a headline, URL, description/call to action. Make sure that the ad is achieving the objective you set before the PPC campaign.
The ads display on the right hand site or the very top of the SERP (before the organic search results).

Here is a sample ad received in response to a search for "remodeling in Chicago." It was the 5th one down on the right.

Bathroom **Remodeling**
www.homewerksinc.net/Bathroom-Gallery
1 (708) 689 1022
Award-winning bathroom design -
Get 30% off & a free consultation!

You can see the bolded keywords are Bathroom Remodeling. There is an offer (30% off). Also, because this is a local business, the local phone number (708 is a suburban Chicago area code) and a link to the website are also in the ad. They also are sending this traffic from this ad to a very specific landing page within their site. This ad has a great chance of getting some quality visits and leads.

You can track your PPC campaign performance by using with stats from your AdWords account and Google analytics software. The results will let you know if adjustments to the ads or keywords are needed. You can also track phone calls from your ads with call tracking numbers and "dynamic insertion". Basically you get your programmer to insert a small piece of code on your landing page using java script and when someone from a paid search campaign lands on your website, your phone number will automatically switch to your call tracking number. It's a great way to track the campaign and see what your real return on investment is. Typically anywhere from 50-80% of your leads will come via the phone and not your web forms, so please take some time to find a way to track your phone leads.

Three key terms related to paid search include:

Conversion rate- The conversion rate to your goal is 10% if your ad gets 200 clicks and 20 purchases are made.

CTR (Click through rate)- This refers to the number of times an ad is clicked divided by the number of times the ad was displayed.

CPC (Cost per click)- This is the amount you pay when a user clicks on your ad.

If you decide to use paid search or PPC as part of your overall marketing strategy, you want to make sure the ads, brief as they are, represent your brand correctly while achieving your marketing goal. You also want to make sure you set a realistic budget and get enough "air-time."

The reasons most PPC campaigns fail for a local business are typically the following:

- **The budget is just too small** and you aren't getting enough impressions to generate sufficient interest. Not getting enough impressions is similar to running a television commercial at 11:00PM on some channel that very few people watch. You just aren't going to get the results you are looking for without running a campaign long enough to get good data to see if it's working or not.

- **You are only using a landing page and have a poor quality main site.** I have seen a lot of campaigns fail where they have a very nice landing page but the rest of the site is terrible. Why is this? For the remodeling markets, your prospects want to read about you and research you. So if you had a nice landing page designed but the rest of your site stinks and/or has very little content, reviews, videos, etc, your chances of landing that lead narrow immensely. If you have a great offer, your results may be better.

- **The rest of your online presence is terrible.** I would caution anyone from investing in a paid search campaign without building a solid web presence first. I have personally tested this many many times and paid search works a lot better if you have a great web presence with quality information everywhere online, good social profiles, at least 10 reviews, a couple of videos, and a really nice website. You are going to be told (sold) differently from all the advertising reps knocking down your door, and you are welcome to test this yourself, but invest in your website/USP/guarantee/web presence first before you invest a ton of money in paid search.

- **No USP and No Guarantee combined with an overall weak offer.** You will not get many leads using paid search if you cannot stand out. And you cannot stand out if you do not have a killer marketing message (USP and Guarantee). You must figure this out before you go throwing money at paid search. Odds are if you have tried paid search before and it didn't work, you haven't applied most of the advice in this book.

- **You are competing against the pros.** No offense, but if you and I were running a paid search campaign for the same type of business in the same local market, you would get crushed by my team. We live and breathe this stuff everyday and are constantly working to improve our craft. Just keep this in mind as you manage your campaigns and do not seem to be getting the results you hoped for. You will need to invest more time in your knowledge of paid search or hire someone who really understands paid search better than anyone else on your team.

Strategy #6 Reputation Marketing and Getting a Reputation Online

What Is Reputation Marketing?

You have probably heard the term "Reputation Management" thrown around a lot these days. This term seems to be the new business buzz phrase yet very few seem to really grasp the role it plays for their remodeling businesses and very few people explain it well at all. I am not a big fan of the term and it's why people need to get away from it and start thinking about Reputation Marketing.

My definition of Reputation Management: It's the practice of understanding, influencing, and managing an individual, business, or brand.

My definition of Reputation Marketing: It's the practice of actively marketing, managing, and promoting a brand consistently online and offline using a variety of strategies to control an entire internet presence including, but not limited to: reviews, social media, local listings, vertical directories, forums, blogs, and a branded website, association sites and the Better Business Bureau.

Everything I am going to share with you about Reputation Marketing is for the sole purpose of helping you grow your local business and learning how to drive new leads from it. I do not want you to waste money and effort on marketing ideas that do not accomplish this for your local business.

I have also written an entire book on this topic as I feel it is probably the most important strategy for local businesses to master in the new economy. (You can check out my new book *"Reputation Marketing Guide for Local Business. How to Power Growth For Your Local Business by Getting a Reputation Online"* at www.ryanpauladams.com/books and on Amazon.)

Reputation Marketing is Competition Crushing...When Done Correctly

Good reputation marketing combined with local listing strategies are what I consider to be "competition crushing" and will help you build a great online presence. I probably spend more time educating and consulting on reputation marketing lately than I do anything else. It has become so important to everything we try to do online for local businesses that a lot of time has to be spent on this. Review sites change rapidly and the process for how they accept reviews also changes. This needs constant attention.

This is one of the main reasons why our first service offering for the clients we work with tends to be getting their reputation and local listings up and running before fixing anything else.

The combination of getting ranked in Google + Local/Maps/Places in addition to having awesome, high quality information about your business online, and lots of good reviews from actual clients produces the highest initial ROI of anything else you can do for online marketing.

Make sure you take a second and understand what I just said. It's really important.

Most of your competitors are not going to do reputation marketing, because they simply do not know how to go about it. They do not see its importance like you do now. Also, most remodeling businesses are simply too scared to invest money in any marketing at all and will continue to squeak by with referrals. They do not have the slightest clue how to market their brand and reputation online. However, you will now be armed with the information to do so.

Put yourself in your consumer's shoes. If you were looking for "roofer in Chicago" and you saw one business with 45 positive reviews and another one with 1 or 2 reviews, who would you choose?

Exactly! Reputation is everything. Your good name is more important than your health.

You want to be the business with 45 positive reviews, and you want the review profiles of your competitors to be a ghost town. And do not be afraid of a couple of negative reviews, they will happen. This is only going to enhance the public perception about your business and I guarantee it will have a positive effect as well on your bottom line.

There really isn't one negative I can think of when it comes to implementing reputation marketing into your business, other than the fact that it can be a pain if you already have some negative reviews, but even then, it's not too late to get on board and get control. Focus on getting new positive reviews to negate the existing bad reviews.

Monitor, influence, and control your business reputation online before it's too late.

The Stats

In case you haven't had the chance yet to see the importance of a having a Positive Online Reputation and local online business presence for your remodeling business, let me show you some stats:

- 90 percent of consumers trust recommendations from others. (**Source: Forrester).** Meaning, they trust what other "reviews" say about your remodeling business. Those Reviews NEED to be positive!

- Traffic to the top 10 review sites grew on average 158% last year **(Source: Compete.com).** Meaning, consumers are going to review sites to learn more about "who to do business with".

- 75 percent of people do not believe that companies tell the truth in advertisements **(Source: Yankelovich).** Meaning, they do not believe you, they believe your prior customers.

You cannot do reputation marketing as a local business without incorporating local search and local search listings. You have to have 100% control over your entire business information across the web, have lots of consistent local listings, and present that information in a professional manner.

Online reputation management became necessary with the advent of social networks, review sites, online forums, blogs and other forms of online communication and information sharing. But since current laws are insufficient and do not prevent total strangers from damaging your online reputation... online reputation management and marketing is now more critical than ever.

Looking Your Professional Best on the Internet

I'll break it down a little more...

Online reputation marketing is the practice of making people and businesses, like yours, look their best on the internet. To accomplish that, people need to control their online search results because they frequently contain inaccurate, misleading or outdated information and listings which can adversely influence how your customers will view you.

Get consistent with your NAP data across all local search sites and directories, provide lots of ways for people to research your company, and lots of ways for past clients to leave reviews. We reviewed this in Strategy #4. Having great data and information all across the web is vitally important to having a consistent/quality reputation to market.

You want a competitive edge over your competition, right? One of the best ways to gain that edge is to have lots of positive, authentic reviews online at a variety of review sites. Your offline customers may know how great you are, but your new prospects have NO clue who you are or what you have done. Getting a reputation online is one of the biggest areas small-medium sized remodeling businesses struggle with. This is by far and away the most important part of your marketing strategy to help convince interested prospects to take the leap to contact and even hire you!

It's not always easy to generate authentic reviews but I will share with you some tips that you can put into action:

- **Set Up and Claim your Review Site Profiles:** Focus on the top review sites for now: Yelp, Google + Local, Yahoo, CitySearch, InsiderPages, YellowPages (YP), SuperPages, and Angie's List. Setup a complete profile with all your business information (again be consistent), images, videos, etc. If you have multiple locations, setup profiles for each location.

- **Link to Your Review Sites:** Encourage reviews by putting your links to your top review profiles on your website, social profiles, and local listings (if that option is available). Sometimes it's as simple as letting people know that you would love to hear what their experience was and making it simple for them to do so. You have to make reviews a focal point of your marketing online.

- **Better Business Bureau:** Remember when I said that clients are terrified of getting burned by contractors or making a bad choice? One of the primary places clients check up on you and your reputation is the Better Business Bureau. Help your clients find peace of mind by getting accredited by the Better Business Bureau and prominently featuring the BBB logo on your site.

- **Ask for a Review including a Video Review:** Did you just finish a job that went well? Set up a process for emailing your past clients and asking for a testimonial or review. Give the client some options as to where they can leave that review. Better yet, ask if they would be willing to give a brief video review in your exit interview. Video reviews are very powerful.

- **Develop a Review Page:** You should offer the ability for clients to also leave reviews directly on your site. A quality programmer or designer can integrate this feature into your site using the "Hreview" rich snippet. This doesn't carry as much weight as a review on a review site, but it is still valuable.

- **Promote Your Existing Reviews:** Do you have some reviews online? Try promoting and sharing those full reviews on your Facebook Fan Page, Twitter, and in your monthly email campaign. There are tons of other options here to promote those. Get creative. You never know who is reading your content and it might just be the reminder your past client needs to post a review.

- **3rd Party Review Collecting:** Hire a 3rd Party to call some of your past prospects that have not left reviews. I would not do this yourself as it becomes a little suspect if you are the one gathering the reviews and posting online. Find a 3rd party service that can transcribe and verify the quality and accuracy of the reviews and also post them online. (Do not risk your online reputation by trying to post these yourself to fake Google or Yelp accounts!)

- **Offline Marketing:** Incorporate a link to your review page on your website in your offline marketing. That review page on your website needs to link to all the review sites you setup. Use it as your central depository of review site possibilities for your past clients. Business cards, thank you notes, invoices...you get the picture. They all should have a short link (something you can track) linking to this review page.

- **ASK!:** Every local service business should be thanking each client at the end of every project. Customers want to feel appreciated and just a simple follow-up phone call goes a long way. Tell them you appreciate their business and ask them if there is anything else you can do. Offer to send them a discount for the next job, ask for referrals, and finally ask if they wouldn't mind leaving a review of their service experience online.

- **Mobile:** If your website is not mobile friendly or you haven't developed a mobile site you are in some trouble at a local level. Remember, 50%+ of Mobile queries are made with local intent. Get your website developer to set you up for mobile.

- **Incentivize:** I left this one as the last on my list because it's my least favorite. You shouldn't have to offer a "$5 Coffee Card for a Review on Yelp" or other incentivized offers to your past customers. It's a poor practice that I do not agree with but I know plenty of businesses that do it. I would try and combine this type of offer into a referral program.

Here is an example of an email I might send out to a previous customer and combine a referral strategy with reputation marketing:

> *Referrals are the greatest testament to what we do! If you know any friends or family that might need our services, for every referral you send us we will give you $150.00 cash.* All we ask in return is that the lead/referral is a valid one and you can email us at info@xyzremodeling.com with the Name, Address, and Phone Number of the referral and we will make every attempt to get a hold of them.*

> *Also, we would love your feedback on our services. Your feedback means the world to us and having you leave a review on our Review Page or our Google + or Yelp page would be great! And for each person who does*

this for us, we will send you a $5 Gift Card to Starbucks. It's a small way for us to show our appreciation.

*List your terms and full details here. Be clear with your offer. Make sure to provide the exact URL of the review profiles you want reviews on!

Your Clients Are Scared Out of Their Mind

We touched on this earlier in the book. Prospects have no idea who to trust when dealing with infrequent purchase decisions. And infrequent purchase decisions describe almost every purchase related to the remodeling industry. Countless numbers of people across the country have been burned by shady contractors. These lousy business owners (if you can call them that) make your life miserable...unless you know how to market and position yourself correctly. Your customers are scared out of their mind when it comes to choosing their next remodeling pro so make it easy and show them you are the clear-cut choice.

To make it even easier for them, make a list of all the negative associations people have with your industry and your service. Get it all out in the open by including them in a Frequently Asked Questions page on your site. You can make it funny, but get your point across that you understand your customer's fears. Talk about it in the open and point out how you handle these concerns.

What can also help you to combat negative industry views is for you to get reviews and testimonials from highly respected people in your community (doctors, nurses, teachers, firefighters, clergy, coaches, etc.). These types of testimonials can provide almost instant credibility for you and brand you as an authority in your market.

How to Deal with Negative Reviews

The longer a negative review actually sits in the search results for a specific keyword, the harder it will be to move down in the rankings. That is another reason that monitoring your reputation is so important. You can catch anything that's fishy or damaging to your business early on, fight it, and put a positive spin on it.

Most review sites let you respond to your reviews. Some of this can be automated in the review site or with reputation management software while some of it has to be done manually. Make sure that every review gets a reply. Start by saying "Thank You" regardless of whether it's a negative or positive review. Too many businesses make the mistake of only responding to the negative reviews, but what does that say to the good customers who took time to leave a nice review? It says that you only value the opinion of the person who is not happy and could not care less about the customer who values your service.

Never fight negativity with negativity. This is a sure fire way for you to come across as a business to stay clear of. The age old motto "the customer is always right" still exists online. Here is how to combat your negative reviews:

- **Thank them for their business.** Customers want to feel appreciated in every transaction they enter into. Do not assume that they feel appreciated or that you did them a favor by doing work for them.

- **Apologize but do not admit fault.** "I am truly very sorry that you were not happy with the service we provided. We strive to be the best at what we do, but we are human and can make mistakes. We stand behind everything we do and one of our service professionals will call you today to attempt to rectify the situation."

- **Make it right!** If you screwed up, get your butt back there and make them happy. If you are dealing with a pain-in-the-you-know-what customer, there might not be a lot you can do but you have to try and make it right.

- **Ask for a retraction.** At the end of the service call, if you feel you have gone above and beyond and have made them happy, ask politely if they could retract their negative review online. You will win more of these than you will lose. Most people do not want to ruin your business and will remove the review or update it to a positive one.

I do not believe in offering a discount on the service you just delivered to get rid of a negative review. There are some sharks out there and they do use reviews as a way to get cash back at the end of the job, even if they were completely satisfied. Make it a policy to do whatever you can do to make them happy, but never give money back.

Good Reviews + Local Search Listings (Citations) = More Traffic, Better Rankings in Local Search

Reputation marketing is GREAT for your traffic and organic keyword rankings. This is often one of the most overlooked benefits of a good reputation marketing strategy and for some could easily be considered the most important.

When Google ranks a business in its Local Search results, the quantity and diversity of online reviews and local listings play a major role. I do not work at Google and do not have access to their search algorithm, but any local search marketing expert will tell you that it's extremely important. If you want more local search traffic, better organic rankings, and higher quality leads get your reputation marketing and local search listings going.

All things being equal, if a competitor's website has the same number of content pages, same number of back-links, and the quality of the site is equal to yours, the website with more reviews and citations will outrank the site with less. This has been proven with results that are related to local intent. Reputation marketing may be the key piece you are missing to get more traffic and leads in local search.

Just keep in mind that it simply does not look natural if all your customers leave reviews on one review site or leave reviews on your website. It looks a bit fishy. So, make sure you encourage reviews on a couple of sites and make it easy for your customers to leave reviews. Consistency is key to avoid any red flags or getting your review site accounts banned. 100 new reviews on one site in one month will appear odd if your closest competitor only has 5 reviews.

Lastly, if you have an office space where your clients meet with you, do not have them leave a review at your office using your internet connection. Most of the review sites are pretty good about tracking where the reviews come from and seeing lots of reviews coming from the same IP Address is a great way to get your review site account banned. Also, do not ever post the reviews yourself for your clients and do not make up fake reviews. You will get caught eventually and your account will get shut down.

Strategy #7- Stay Connected: Lead With Value and Automate Your Follow Up

Automate Your Lead Nurturing and Retention:

If you already have a great web presence for your remodeling business and are currently getting lots of traffic and leads from different marketing sources, you are most likely in a great position to double sales in the next 6-12 months by automating your lead nurturing and retention strategy. Yes, that's right! You can DOUBLE sales in the next 6-12 months by implementing this.

Retention (stay in front of past clients) and lead automation (staying in front of your top prospects) is actually something that I have struggled with for years and put it off because I just did not have time and felt it was too complicated to implement. Boy was I wrong! Once you have the right system in place, you can let it do most of the work for you. It takes on average 5-7 messages to reach your prospect before they really pay attention to you.

There are several great solutions out there to help you implement and manage automatic follow-up and retention marketing. It's just a matter of find the right software for your business. It takes a little bit of time and effort to get it setup properly, but this is not something any business should go without.

Getting a new lead is only about 1/2 the battle. That prospect wants to be nurtured and you have to do a better job than your competitors at positioning you or your company as the expert after you get the lead. I do not care if you are a siding contractor, roofer, or water damage remediation company; you need to develop a series of automated follow up "touches" to let your prospect know the following:

- Appreciation - Thank them for requesting more information, an estimate, a free consulting session, etc.

- Next Steps - Let them know what the next steps will be (phone call, series of emails, questionnaire, etc.).

- Confirmation - Let them know they made the right choice by choosing your company and why you are different and unique. Restate your USP and Unique Guarantee here!

- Information - Be the clear expert in your industry by providing great information after the conversion and on a monthly basis (Top 5 Questions to Ask Your Roofer, 3 Key Things to Look for When Choosing a Siding Product, etc.).

Use both email and direct mail for lead follow up and retention. The simplest way is to generate an email follow up sequence is by using software that can do this for you.

Personally, I love Infusionsoft and think it's a great tool for remodeling contractors. I also believe that companies like MarketSharp and ImproveIt 360! offer a great remodeling focused CRM that can help you automate your marketing and your business. You can learn more about my recommended resources by going to www.PME360.com/resources.

Do not forget to create another automated follow up sequence for those clients who you just finished a job for. Clients want to feel appreciated every time they give you their hard earned money. You are not doing them a favor no matter how much money (or lack thereof) you charged them for your work. Send them a handwritten thank you note, birthday card, and other direct mail and email messages after the sale to show them you are still thinking about and appreciate them.

Your competitors are not doing any of this for their current leads and past clients. It can be a game changer for your business.

There are many ways you can nurture prospects and get more referrals and have the entire process 90%-100% automated. I love Infusionsoft for integrating nurturing systems, but there is a lot of good software out there that can help you do this including a simple email marketing software like Aweber or Constant Contact.

Lead With Value and Create a "7 Things You Should Know Guide", "Top 10 Questions You Should Ask", or "Design Trends Guide"

Every remodeling contractor needs to have standards built into their business and their marketing. You have certainly thought about this but now it's time to get all of your standards and processes into writing.

Over the past 2 years, my team and I at PME 360 have been working on creating and integrating a "7 Things You Should Know Before Hiring_____ in <Insert City>" into each one of our exclusive clients' marketing systems *(if you would like to see a sample, simply request a Free Strategy Session at the end of this book and we can show you some samples).* This is a key part of our delay the sale strategy and it flat out works!

Most of our clients have experienced at least a 2x's increase in leads captured by leading with a free report like this have also increase their close ratios significantly. We do not recommend removing your free estimate or consultation from your website or process as that would be a mistake. But offering multiple pieces of bait to attract your ideal client to you is critical to the success of any marketing campaign.

But as I have stated before, just about anyone can drive traffic and leads but very few marketers can design campaigns that attract ideal clients, weed out the tire kickers, take pressure off of the sales teams, dramatically improve overall close ratio, and allow you to sell at a premium price (More from Less). This is the goal you should be striving for in when designing your marketing system.

Do not wait until your first face to face sales meeting with your prospect to get something into their hands. It needs to happen right after the lead comes in and all of this can be automated with the right tools and process.

Here is what your "Hire Me Guide" should include:

- An Introduction (why should anyone hire you?)
- History of the Company
- Photos of the Key People in Your Company
- Licenses and Insurance Information
- Reviews and Testimonials
- Before and After Pictures of Your Best Projects

- Awards, Association Memberships, References
- Explain Your Process from Estimate to Doing the Work
- Sample Contract (Optional)
- Conduct Expected of Your Team
- Restate Your USP & Guarantee
- Frequently Asked Questions
- Conclusion
- Restate Your Call to Action

You can also include a Checklist of some kind for visual help in differentiating your company from your top competitors. The guide should clearly be authored by the key person in your company like the President or CEO and this persons picture should be right on the front of the guide. Adding this personal touch is a proven technique that leads to a higher response rate and helps make it more personal.

Once you develop this a graphic designer or word processing expert can help put this into a nice digital and print brochure for you to upload to your website (do not give people access to this document directly, make them request information from you before sending this to them).

Now that you have the "Hire Me Guide" created and the FAQ section, use this to create another 1-2 page document titled "Top 10 Questions You Should Ask a Roofer" or whatever remodeling niche you are in. And really think about the top 10 concerns that every prospect has when looking to hire someone to do work at their house. Put this into a document and you have created another killer handout and content that can be placed on your website to capture more business.

The biggest concerns most prospects have in this industry typically come down to how long is it going to take, who is going to be in my home, how messy are they/you going to be, what happens if a mistake is made, how long will you stand behind your service/products, and lastly.....cost. Notice that I did not put cost first because it is not the #1 concern. Address everything else and differentiate yourself and price will not be an issue.

Next, you can slice and dice this content you just created and integrate this into your automated nurturing email sequence, use some of this content for a 3-step direct mail campaign to those prospects that haven't hired you yet, create some new pages of content on your website, and print them out and hand out to prospects in your first meeting.

This is not a sales pitch, but PME 360 can do all of this for you along with creating high converting landing pages for this front end guide offer and integrating all of this into your existing website. PME 360 will also create the email nurturing sequence with proven high converting copy and handle all of the automation sequences. Go to www.PME360.com/leadengine to learn more.

Be Proactive with Your Prospects and Especially Those That You Have Done an Estimate or Consultation For

The absolute worst thing in the world is investing time with someone who you feel is a quality prospect and doing a free estimate (or even a paid one) and not getting the job. First of all, please do not do free estimates with the hope and pray method – "I really hope and pray that if I do this free estimate that the price will be right for them and they will hire me."

Even those contractors who have great sales processes still get burned by tire kickers and those who are only looking for the cheapest quote. Be aware and stop investing your time into people who aren't committed to you financially. Flat out, free estimates are a terrible business strategy and completely kill your positioning and time.

Estimates waste a lot of valuable time and should only be used after a consultation, and maybe not at all. Stop doing free estimates and if you are going to do a free estimate, make it more of a free consultation or project review where you ask lots of great questions. Asking lots of great questions will quickly reveal if the person(s) sitting in front of you are a good fit for you or not. This should all be part of a consistent sales process.

Now, if you do free estimates or project consultations as part of your sales process to land a new job, please make sure you are following up with that prospect. These are big ticket sales and you should be able to afford to send them something really nice in the mail a day or two after you send them the estimate or project consultation.

Emailing them is weak. Calling them is better. Inviting them to a special event is even better. But the #1 strategy you should be implementing in your post estimate and consultation process is direct mail in combination with some automated nurturing as described in this chapter.

No matter what you send in the mail, make sure you include a handwritten personalized note or letter. This will go a long way and your competition is not doing this.

Here are some ideas for direct mail (3D or lumpy mail) pieces you can send after the estimate or consultation:

- **Send them a copy of your book:** Yes! You should consider writing a book. You would be the only person in your local market that has authored a book and this would give you a huge step up on your competitors.
- **Send them a gift:** Thank them for considering you and show them you appreciate them even before you do business. This will plant a major seed in their mind that if this is what you do before they are even a client, they can only imagine how well you would treat them during and after becoming a client.
- **Personalized video message:** There are several direct mail companies out there that can help you develop a personalized video book that you can mail. Connect the book to your computer, upload a quick 2-5 minute personalized video and send in the mail.
- **Personalized Message in a Blueprint Tube:** This works really well for those in the custom whole house remodeling, additions, or home building business. Send them a really cool message, sample design, or something creative in a large blueprint tube and mail it. This will certainly grab their attention.
- **Anything lumpy:** Lumpy or bulky mail gets opened so brainstorm some different things you can send in the mail that are 3-D.

I hope you get the idea and I could go on forever with direct mail ideas for this industry. The point here is that you cannot just leave an estimate out there and hope that they hire you. You need to go after that business and that needs to come from multiple places with direct mail being the most important. If you believe 100% in what you do this shouldn't be a problem. Be a pest but be nice. Be memorable and you will earn more business from the leads you are already getting.

Conclusion

The money is out there in the remodeling market and it is not going away. Baby boomers and their children are in position to inherit $27 trillion over the next 4 decades (**Source: WSJ**) and are going to invest in all kinds of goods and services related to remodeling. That's why I personally love the remodeling industry and feel it's positioned for some of the biggest growth ever seen.

If you do all of what I have outlined in this book there is NO competition. None. Especially in your local market. People are lazy and won't go through the trouble of creating and implementing all of this. Competition levels (perceived or real) are only going to get tighter if you are doing and saying the same thing as everyone else. And even if you are in a market competing with the Top 100 Remodelers, you can be smarter and nimbler than they can be. Innovate. Differentiate. Implement and you will succeed.

To grow your remodeling business you need to implement all or most of the strategies listed in this book. This is no easy task and it's difficult to implement all of these strategies on your own. The question becomes should you do this yourself, hire someone in-house, or outsource? If you are a bigger company, a combination of all three is probably the best choice. That said, **I still believe that outsourcing all of your online marketing to a quality agency is not only possible, but it's the best way to leverage your time and internal resources.**

If you have read this far, you are now knowledgeable enough to start asking the right questions of your internal team, agency, or use this book to develop a job description to hire the right team of people.

Keep in mind hiring one person to do all of this is difficult - if not impossible. Finding one person who understands how to craft compelling selling propositions and guarantees, understands direct response marketing, copywriting, SEO, local SEO, PPC, landing pages, automation funnels, programming, social media, blogging, software, etc. is very very rare. I only know of a few and they are not cheap.

You are probably better off finding a team or agency like PME 360 that has people already in place that are experts in each one of these areas. It's faster to implement, get set up, and start seeing results. The results and impact typically are dramatically better than anything else you could attempt on your own unless you are willing to invest the time.

Lastly, all knowledge and marketing systems aren't created equal. Look for a team or person who understands your business, your industry, and the specific challenges you face. It will make a big difference in the end. Don't hire a generalist.

If you implement even just 40-50% of the 7 strategies and additional concepts I have laid out in this book I guarantee that you can become the leader in your local remodeling market.

If you do all of the above even just marginally well you will succeed but it won't happen overnight. Getting all of this right takes hard work and testing and tweaking to get it right. It does not have to be perfect, just good enough or better than your competition. Learn some basic copy writing or hire an expert to do it for you. Implement a track and measure strategy and be everywhere your clients are.

You Have to Believe You are Worth It

Too many people just do not believe they can become wealthy and believe they just are not worth it. Remodeling contractors score notoriously low on the self worth scale and many have very low self esteem. I do not know why this is exactly but this is another thing that has to change now.

You are providing an incredible service and solving some very complicated problems for people. You are important and you are worth every penny of what you are charging and should probably be charging a lot more. I have dedicated my life to helping this industry because I believe that the work you are doing is extremely important.

Have confidence in yourself and integrate an entrepreneurial mindset that starts with marketing first and you will be successful. It is the only way out of the chaos of your business. There is so much money out there and tons of people looking for the services you offer.

Now get yourself in position to attract those people and capture a small slice of that $127 trillion.

Ryan Paul Adams...A Little History

Baseball- The Early Dream

Ever since I was 14-years old, I have been in business and when I was 15, I started working in my family's remodeling and home building venture.

But being a pretty good baseball player, I went to college to pursue my dream of playing in the big leagues. (My father saved all the messages from the scouts that used to call.) Unfortunately, a gruesome ankle injury ended that dream far too quickly; however, it didn't kill my drive. I wanted to apply the grit and determination I used in sports to the real world, so I went back to working in the family business; this time, with a wholehearted vigor.

Back in Remodeling

I devoured everything I could get my hands on related to remodeling, marketing, business, sales, finance, growing a business, and the internet. I was learning, applying what I learned and working really long hours. It soon became apparent, however, that filling all the positions our company needed with the few people we had would lead to burnout. Especially with me doing much of the work myself.

The Internet Jump Starts Success

One area I stayed with was the internet. On some level, I sensed that the web held a lot of promise for our business. At the time, though, very few local businesses had websites and the cost to get one professionally done was astronomical. I took that on and learned everything I could about internet marketing, building a website, conversion, and search engine optimization.

I quickly understood the power that search engines were going to have on local businesses as I began applying what I learned. The leads started to come in. First it was one per week. Then, it was three to five per week. Soon, during some weeks we were getting several leads per day. The flow was one thing but the quality of the leads was as good as the referrals we were getting. We were landing deals of $50k, $150k, $300k and even got our first million dollar deal from the internet for our remodeling and home building business!

We began achieving real success and had become an established remodeler but I wanted more. I desired to embrace my own destiny, so, I began looking at developing a subdivision. I wanted to make the "BIG" money, or so I thought….

The Much Fabled Land of Milk and Honey

"No great entrepreneur has achieved great success without great failure. I have failed, succeeded, failed again, and succeeded again. It's not from your successes that you learn the most; it's from your failures. You learn the fastest from those ideas, clients, and business deals that didn't work out. The key is to not repeat your mistakes and have the ability to leap two steps forward each time you are knocked one step back. That is what I have been able to do and what I have taught my clients to do as well."- Ryan Paul Adams

While working in my family remodeling business, we had developed a distinctive selling proposition and a unique guarantee. Online marketing was driving our growth, and with a strong reputation combined with a consistent lead flow, we were doing really well.

I had just built my first house for my wife and me to live in. I was making lots of money and taking great vacations (when we had the time). I bought my first new car, and the momentum was rolling. At 24-years old, I had the nicest house on the block and was on my way...until our lives forever changed course.

A Terrible Business Deal Changed My Life Forever

I became convinced that I could make more money, easier, by developing land, building the home and selling it for a huge profit. The real estate market was solid and I had been just introduced to an area real estate developer who seemed like just the guy to take us to the much fabled land of milk and honey.

Without going into too much detail (someday, I will someday explain everything that happened), we were taken for a ride. I look back and cringe at all the mistakes I made with the deal. It quickly turned into a nightmare, bringing us to dire financial straits. The stress it brought on my family, especially my father, was something I never want to see happen to anyone. It was simply brutal.

While continuing to run the family business, I sold insulation, started an eBay venture (I did $20k in one day on eBay), dabbled in real estate, and did what I could to survive. At this time, my father and I could no longer afford to take salaries as we began clawing our way out of the real estate mess we had gotten into. (In hindsight, if I had just stayed focused on the remodeling business, we would have been fine, but stress has a way of clouding the mind.)

When I'm Onto Something, I'm All In

I continued to pursue my knowledge in the world of internet marketing and web design but it was tough. I was completely burnt out by all that I was doing in the real estate/insulation/remodeling/home building/and eBay world.

I needed a change.

Through all of this, I never lost sight of the enormous potential of the internet and its impact on local businesses. I began to think that with the knowledge I had acquired from day after day of sitting into the wee hours of the night in front of my computer, I could help other small businesses grow using the internet.

I ended up scraping together some funds using an equity loan against my house and untapped credit card balances (that's what credit is there for, right?) to buy an existing internet marketing agency. I took a huge calculated risk to do what I felt was necessary not only to survive but to begin thriving again. Between my wife (being one of the smartest people I know, graduating with a Marketing BA from Simmons) and myself, I already had the genesis of a great team.

The Internet New Business Venture Begins to Thrive

I purchased the business a month after my wife quit her job and we had our first child. A collision of three major life events! Talk about pressure. To add to that, I didn't know the first thing about running an agency. After all, this was a whole new area for me. I needed to learn to make a go of it - fast.

Realizing that I needed to build a quality team around me to grow beyond myself and my wife, I found some awesome people who were as intrigued as I was about the prospect of transforming the lives of small business owners and remodeling companies.

My brother in law, Ron Rodi, took the lead in bringing in new clients in Chicago. So, while most of our clients were in the Windy City (thanks to Ron), we had production running out of Portland, ME. In fact, without Ron, we probably wouldn't have made it. The same could be said for Bryan, Pat, and Katharine – the rest of the PME 360 team. They are among the smartest people I know. I am so grateful that I found them! I couldn't do what I do without them.

Despite living very frugally that first year, there were months we would have missed the mortgage payment unless we landed another client.

But guess what happened?

Effort is a Powerful Force

Every time we needed something big to happen, it did. Effort is a powerful force that generates incredible momentum once it gets rolling. If you stick with it and apply effort consistently you will succeed. I tend to apply more than just a normal amount of effort, though. That's why I feel that I have quickly become one of the top consultants in the remodeling and home building industry. (Please allow me just this little boast because of the amount of time I have invested in this.)

Within 12 months, we were profitable. I was able to take a salary, quit everything else I was doing and focus on growing our internet marketing agency, PME 360. Within 24 months, we were bringing in upwards of $50,000 a month in revenue and growing fast. Running an internet marketing agency has easily been the hardest thing I have ever done. Far more difficult than when I worked several jobs in that prior rough patch. In fact, it's damn hard.

But I love helping my clients achieve real success in their businesses.

Complete Domination of Local Markets and Hundreds of Websites Later

Somewhere between then and now, we have built and managed hundreds of websites and marketing campaigns. My team and I have developed some of the best marketing systems on the planet. We have achieved incredible results time after time and have helped consistently grow businesses in some of the most insanely competitive markets in the world.

And most important to me, I have an awesome family (thanks Mom and Dad!), two kids and a great wife who supports my tireless work ethic and the ups and downs of running a rapidly growing company and consulting enterprise.

I have consulted with many different types of businesses including Fortune 50, 100, and 500 companies. Being the somewhat introverted and private person that I am, that is not what I prefer to do.

Big companies aren't easy to deal with. It takes forever for most of them to make a decision. They typically want blood from your first born before they will hire you and that is not something I am interested in donating just to land a client.

I work with SMBs (Small-Medium Businesses) in the remodeling and home building industry because if I help you generate an additional $1,000,000 this year I have directly, positively impacted your life. If I do that for a large franchise or big company it goes almost completely unnoticed and unappreciated.

That's my story and I am sticking to it!

Ryan Paul Adams has been in the remodeling business for over 15 years and President and CEO of PME 360 for 8 years. The combination of the two experiences has made him a go-to person in the remodeling industry when it comes to attracting and retaining clients. Ryan has been featured in Forbes Magazine (May 2015), Americas Premier Experts, Remodeling Magazine Online, Daily5 Remodel, Boston Globe, Yahoo Finance, Los Angeles Daily News, and The Street.

You can find him at www.PME360.com

P.S. Limited Time Offer - Free Strategy Session

To be honest, I do not know how long I can offer this so I would recommend requesting a free strategy session with me as soon as possible. I know I won't be able to offer this for much longer as my time is becoming more and more limited.

You can contact me for a free strategy session at: www.PME360.com/invitation or call my direct line 24/7 at 1-888-997-6336 Ext 711.

Notes

[1] Scott DeGarmo, "The Success Issue," *Success Magazine*, nd.

[2] National Association of Home Builders, "Remodeling Market Index (RMI)," April 25, 2013. http://www.nahb.org/fileUpload_details.aspx?contentID=137354

[3] Craig Webb, "Top 100 Markets," *Remodeling Magazine,* February 2013. http://www.remodeling.hw.net/rri/top-100-markets.aspx

[4] Mary H.J. Farrell, "Remodeling Activity is Highest in Seven Years, According to Key Measure," *Consumer Reports,* November 12, 2012. http://homes.yahoo.com/news/remodeling-activity-is-highest-in-seven-years--according-to-key-measure.html

[5] Jakob Nielsen and Kara Pernice, "Eyetracking Web Usability," 2010.

[6] Myles Anderson, "The Building Blocks of Good Local SEO," *Search Engine Land,* October 12, 2012. http://searchengineland.com/the-building-blocks-of-good-local-seo-137825

[7] Constant Contact, "SinglePlatform Survey: Nearly Half of Local Businesses Never Update Their Online Listings," February 5, 2013. http://news.constantcontact.com/press-release/singleplatform-survey-nearly-half-local-businesses-never-update-their-online-listings

[8] Constant Contact, "SinglePlatform Survey."

[9] Stephanie Hobbs, "5 Areas that Demonstrate the Growing Potential of Local Search," *Search Engine Land,* November 12, 2012. http://searchengineland.com/growing-potential-of-local-search-demonstrated-in-new-survey-139274

[10] Ed Parsons, "Using Location Data for Business: Past, Present and Future," [presented at Google PinPoint London 2012, October 17, 2012]. http://lanyrd.com/2012/google-pinpoint-london/scgtgr/

[11] Oliver St John, "Study: Social Media a Bust for Small Businesses," *USA Today,* April 17, 2013. http://www.usatoday.com/story/money/personalfinance/2013/04/16/small-business--social-media-facebook/2075123/

Made in the
USA
Middletown, DE